YOUTUBE STRATEGIES 2015

How To Make And Market YouTube Videos That
Bring Hungry Online Buyers Straight To Your
Products And Services

Paul Colligan
www.YouTubeStrategiesBook.com

ISBN-13: 978-1514139615
ISBN-10: 1514139618

Disclaimer

I create commercial content that pays bills. I am, what many would call, an information marketer.

Often, I am the provider (and/or business owner) of the products and/or services that I recommend. Being in this business provides me with such a wonderful opportunity; it's part of how I pay those bills.

Occasionally, I am compensated by the products and services I recommend. It is sometimes direct; it is sometimes indirect; but it is there.

If this offends you, no problem; this isn't content for you. Return this book. We can still be friends.

At all times, I only recommend products I use – or would tell my Mom to use. You have my promise there.

About The Author

Paul Colligan helps others leverage technology to expand their reach (and revenue) with reduced stress and no drama. He does this with a lifestyle and business designed to answer the challenges and opportunities of today's ever-changing information economy. If you are looking for titles, he is a husband, father, 7-time best-selling author, podcaster, keynote speaker and CEO of Colligan.com. He lives in Portland, Oregon with his wife and daughters and enjoys theater, music, great food and travel.

Paul believes in building systems and products that work for the user – not vice versa. With that focus, he has played a key role in the launch of dozens of successful web and internet products that have garnered tens of millions of visitors in traffic and dollars in revenue. Previous projects have included work with The Pulse Network, Traffic Geyser, Rubicon International, Piranha Marketing, Microsoft and Pearson Education. In addition, he's helped dozens of authors launch their books into bestsellers on Amazon, Podcasters to #1 at iTunes, and has been the secret weapon behind millions of video views at YouTube. Topics of passion include (but are not limited to): new media content creation, multicasting, product development, and lifestyle design.

Paul's unique take on the internet can be seen, heard and read on web shows, including The Podcast Report; books, including the Kindle Bestsellers Cross Channel Social Media Marketing, How To Podcast 2015 and YouTube Strategies 2015; as well as several publications, both on and offline, as varied as the Huffington Post and The Net Effect. He is a popular speaker on internet technology topics and frequently speaks online, on the air and before audiences about his passions. He has presented at events around the world that which include BlogWorld and New Media Expo, The European Business Podcasting Summit, Google Tech Talks, MacWorld, Social Media Success Summit, Inbound Marketing Summit, Social Media Marketing World and Microsoft Tech-Ed.

If you are interested in his latest projects and/or thoughts on the industry that has been so good to him, there is plenty more to read, watch, and ponder at www.PaulColligan.com.

Table Of Contents

About This Book

"Successful people ask better questions, and as a result, they get better answers." Tony Robbins

When the previous versions of YouTube Strategies went to #1 and continued to sell impressive numbers and earn great reviews, I knew this book had it's place in the marketplace dialog. To my past readers and supporters, I can't thank you enough.

Why the update for 2015? We continue to see a rapid maturation at YouTube in areas that should be part of any YouTube strategy - at any level. Some of these elements weren't in the first book - or even in last year's edition. They are added in this one.

In my history of producing internet training , I've taken pride in creating content that lasted. YouTube changes so quickly that I find myself having to delete numerous training videos before I can ever publish them.

This book is partially a way to deal with that frustration. There are the specifics of YouTube, which need videos and screenshots - and there are the Strategies of YouTube, which I examine here. This is, in short, a book of questions and answers - the questions that you should be asking about YouTube and the real answers that will help you put together a strategy for YouTube that makes sense to you and your business. This is meant to be the reference guide you have by your side as you figure out what to do with all of the options and all of the changes as you plan your own, personal,

YouTube Strategies .

In many cases, you don't need one chapter to make sense of a previous one. They are as self-contained (and short) as possible - unless otherwise noted. Feel free to skip around.

Although every chapter has been updated in one way or another, there are a several brand new chapters that deal with the new features YouTube has brought our way in the last year. Included in the list is YouTube Cards, paid channels, sponsorship rule changes and the introduction of some new video creation tools.

I also reordered the chapters in this book to to better reflect a strategic approach to YouTube. We start with making videos and then move into publishing them. From there, I offer strategies for marketing the videos and then look at a number of advanced strategies that should be considered by anyone looking to take YouTube seriously.

At the time of writing, YouTube reports seeing 300 hours of video uploaded to their site every single minute (this number is up from 100 hours just last year). I'm sure by the time this book goes to press, the number will go up again.

Also according to YouTube (as of April 2015):

1. YouTube has more than 1 billion users

2. Every day people watch hundreds of millions of hours on YouTube and generate billions of views

3. The number of hours people are watching on YouTube each month is up 50% year over year

Source - https://www.youtube.com/yt/press/

So, with these changes, I am re-releasing this book updated for 2015. At its core are the top questions I get asked about YouTube - as well as a few that people should be asking. I am still asked these questions on a regular basis and I am still convinced that any YouTube strategy should begin with a clear understanding of how YOU need to answer these questions in your own YouTube efforts.

I also offer some additional thoughts about what's next at YouTube and offer a few additional chapters on the topics of automated tools for YouTube marketing and video creation and how to produce the best possible looking videos - no matter what your budget may be.

This is not a Book About the Tech of YouTube!

My goal is to teach you that with YouTube, a "Ready, Aim, Fire" approach is the best. I've seen too many people "Fire" first... and the results are never good.

This is a book of YouTube Strategies - how to think about YouTube, how to understand what you are getting yourself into, and how to use the strategies to "start right." Understand what you are doing first, before you take on the tech.

This book is the "Ready" and "Aim" part. If you were looking for "Fire," no worries, we can still be friends - go ahead and return the book. I'll be okay.

This is not a Book of Only my Content and Ideas

I have a number of bonus chapters in this book that bring a well-rounded examination of all things YouTube. The authors are the best of the best, and it's an honor to have them in this book. In these pages you'll read amazing content from the likes of Mike Koenigs, Mike Stewart, Gideon Shalwick, Travis Shields and Phil Starkovich.

I couldn't more thrilled to have their contributions in this book.

I Will Continue to Update the Book to Include Whatever Changes YouTube Makes this Year

Below I have directions for registering your version of this book. The screens might change. The interface might get gussied up. The strategies I cover, however, probably won't change at all.

Fair enough?

If you'd like to register your book so I can keep you up to date when we make changes (and, with YouTube, you know it will be often), take a look at -

http://www.YouTubeStrategiesBook.com

The registration process is explained there. It's obviously not required, but it is the only way I can keep you up to date.

Thoughts / comments? I'd love to hear them:

http://PaulColligan.com/YouTube

http://PaulColligan.com/GooglePlus

http://PaulColligan.com/Amazon

http://PaulColligan.com/Twitter

http://PaulColligan.com/Facebook

http://YouTubeStrategiesBook.com

Paul Colligan

Portland, Oregon

YouTube Strategies 2015 Version 1.1

What is the Ideal Length for a YouTube Video?

People ask me this all the time: what is the ideal video length? You hear (silly) statements such as, "We are in the YouTube era, nobody watches video more than three minutes." People make these blanket statements of absolute nonsense, so let's take the time to walk through these myths.

Fact: the concept that people only watch short videos online is simply false.

If you think about it logically, YouTube has spent millions of dollars putting up full-length concerts, all-day festivals and other all-day events; simply because people do consume long-form content. They also put up a lot of political events, speeches and debates that are all consumed in great quantities. YouTube would not spend millions putting up long-form content if people didn't watch it.

The reason why most videos are only three minutes in length is because most people only have three minutes of content to say. Or, they are building videos for an audience with three-minute attention spans. If you only have three minutes of content to say, and you have an audience with a three-minute attention span, obviously deal with that audience; but the idea that only short videos are consumed is absolutely ridiculous.

If you want to leave the world of YouTube, consider Hulu, which has hour-long television shows, or Netflix, with feature length films. People are willing (and happy) to consume full-length content online if it is good. Do you think HBO would have launched their stand alone Internet service this year if long form content wasn't something people are looking for?

Truth be told, my most profitable video to date is over an hour and twenty minutes in length and has been viewed more than 50, 100 times. YouTube Analytics tells me my audience retention is better than average for most of the video and I hope to do more like that one in the future.

So what is the ideal video length? How long should you make your video?

The answer is actually quite simple: make your video as long as it needs to be and not one minute longer. The fact of the matter is, you have to know your audience to make that decision. You have to know what it is they are looking for and you have to deliver the right content for them. Understand that they can click out – they can go anywhere they want – and that there are a myriad of competitors for the very piece of information you are trying to stream on YouTube. For that reason, the video needs to be as long as it needs to be; and not one minute – actually, not one second – longer.

So what are the action items? What can you do?

It's an interesting era that we are in – with massive hard drives, unlimited upload space, and the ability to send hours of video to YouTube – and we do often tend to go longer than we need to. Your action item is easy: don't.

When producing your video, figure out exactly what you have to say; and more importantly, figure out exactly what you don't need to say. Then, say only what it is that you need to say, and say it very quickly.

Also, what happens after a video is consumed? Make that part of the content; but again, do that quickly.

Another tip for you is to tell your viewer how long your video is up front; it helps tremendously. What would you rather watch, a video called "Social Media Marketing" or a video called "Social Media Marketing Explained in 3 Minutes and 7 Seconds?" Think about it; I've got three minutes so I'll give that a go. So it can be a strategic implementation, but don't worry about going longer if you need to.

Serve your audience; don't worry about a magic number.

What Equipment and Software Do I Need to Create a Decent Quality Video?

First, you need a high-definition (HD) camera. The funny thing is that the high-definition camera on your phone is probably good enough for what you need to do. And while the HD camera on your phone is good, you can get even better ones for less than $100. In the grand scheme of things, this will probably be the last year I mention that your camera must be HD as it is simply becoming the standard.

Actually, more important than the video is the audio quality. I've seen people who have $50 phone cameras, but $200 or $400 audio rigs, because the audio is actually more important than the camera image.

Do you need that high-definition camera? Yes, you do, because you want to upload in high-definition quality to YouTube so that the consumer takes you seriously. Even so, audio is still more important. There are several great microphones for under $100; you can do your homework by visiting a site like Amazon and looking for the most highly-ranked equipment. My favorite options are listed in the "Paul's Favorite Tech" chapter of this book.

The next most important thing is the lighting; you want to have great lighting. If you can afford it, examine three-point lighting, which you can search for in your favorite search engine (YouTube has video after video that explains how to utilize this method).

One alternative, if you don't have good lighting, is to go outside to Mother Nature where there is good organic lighting (though obviously, don't go out shooting in the middle of a storm). However, know that lighting is the second most important aspect of your video production behind audio.

A decent quality video option can also be a screencast video, which is a video recording of your screen. Screencasting is a technique commonly used in how-to videos. The video that I initially created for this book was a screencast video that's been extremely profitable for me. With screencasting, I don't have to worry about lighting, I don't have to worry about cameras, I just need software and a microphone. It is certainly a great option for you.

The microphone I use is the Blue Nessie, purchased for under $100 on Amazon. In terms of screencasting programs, you have two major software options: Camtasia on the PC and ScreenFlow on the Mac. Both of those programs have 30-day trials that you can utilize if you wish, and you can produce great videos with them. They even have the ability to input video editing if that's something you need.

Finally, in terms of traditional video editing, iMovie on the Mac works well. Whatever version of iMovie you have is great, and you can download it from the Apple store. If you are unfortunate and saddled with a PC, I would not recommend Windows Movie Maker. Sony Movie Studio on the PC, however, is a fine product; and you can usually get that with a coupon for under $100.

What about the higher-end video editing products? Right now, my recommendation is that once you need that kind of work, hand it over to a professional - or consider looking for a book on video editing (versus on one YouTube Strategies).

So the action item is simply to get over the tech and grab a high-definition camera for under $100; or, alternatively, realize that most likely, your phone will do the job. Next, invest in decent audio, set up quality lighting and get to work on making your videos. Then put them on YouTube and see what kind of response you get. There is no better way to pay for a new camera than from the monetary success of your previous videos.

That's all the equipment and software you need to make a decent quality video. Get to work!

Ultra HD? 4K Video?

In the "What's Next" chapter I talk about the new 4K, or Ultra HD, video standard. There are some cameras that you can buy right now that offer that level of quality at some surprisingly reasonable prices. At this point, editing 4K is a considerable undertaking that is not to be underestimated. Consider your comfort and ability level with significantly larger files and make that decision accordingly.

In short, you can produce stunning video with a good HD camera and a decent microphone - quite possibly using the phone in your pocket and a microphone you pick up for less than a hundred bucks.

How Should I Use YouTube Annotations?

Note: YouTube launched a technology this year similar to Annotations called "Cards." We chat about Cards in the next chapter.

You've probably seen YouTube annotations: pop-ups; text bubbles; links; all in different colors and fonts, and all part of the YouTube system. YouTube is working diligently, spending millions of dollars to integrate this across all of the platforms, including television and mobile.

What do you do with that? How do you use them? How do you make them part of your business?

Fact number one: annotations bring integration, they bring interactivity, and they bring some very cool things into the online video process. You definitely want to leverage that.

Fact number two: YouTube is adding more and more features all the time, and they are working diligently in making it work across all of their platforms. YouTube is focused on letting you do more cool things with them on more platforms than ever before.

Some people won't be able to see or interact with annotations, however, so you need to keep that in consideration. Realize that right now, at least at the time of writing, you can even add an annotation that says, "Click here to get a million dollars", but if that person is watching on an iPhone, they won't see the annotation and they won't click for the cash. People on mobile devices just aren't able to use annotations, so take that in consideration during the production of your videos.

So what can you do with annotations? You can obviously incorporate humor, as well as commentary and supplemental things that aren't 100% necessary. You can ask somebody to subscribe or make a joke by telling them when the next video is coming out. Annotations that work best are ones have no negative impact if they are not seen (like when they're viewed on a mobile or another screen).

One thing you can do is you can link – and that's a powerful facet of annotations. At the time of writing, you are able to link to other YouTube videos. Imagine that somebody has just found your Channel and they're watching a video that they like; when they reach the end of the video and they want more, you should certainly tell them, "I have more, here's a video about X". The great thing about annotations is that when viewers click on one, it takes them directly to that video.

I've seen people who have added annotations to their videos and doubled their viewing figures just over the course of one week.

You can also link to a playlist, simply by saying, "If you like this video, I've got ten more videos on this topic," and provide a link to that list. You should realize as well that the playlist can come up in YouTube results, so you have effectively double power there.

You can also link viewers back to your channel page. By providing a channel link, you link people back to who it is you are and what it is you do. It's very powerful and very easy, and I definitely recommend that you do that.

You can also add an annotation to a Google+ profile page. In fact, Google Talk, Google, YouTube, Google Docs – all of the Google empire – tightly integrate with the Google+ social platform. So if you build the link outside of YouTube to your Google+ profile page, it is incredibly powerful. It will bring people to additional content and additional sites and from there, you can link to a subscription button.

Getting people to subscribe to your YouTube Channel is incredibly beneficial and something that you want to consider; because the more people subscribed, the more people will come back when you put up the next video. It begins to be a snowball rolling down the side of the mountain; it gets bigger and bigger with the power of gravity that comes along with it.

You can also link to a fund-raising project for non-profits or to a Kickstarter account.

And finally, there is an option to include annotation links to merchandise providers. YouTube has a list of ones that you can use, so do check the list. At the time of publication, the only e-commerce option available is Shopify (http://www.PaulColligan.com/Shopify), which currently has a 14-day free trial worth looking at.

So, it is possible to link to many cool things external to YouTube; just be aware of the people who are not able to view them.

What are the action items? What can you do with all these choices?

Make use of annotations when they make sense. For example, including a subscribe annotation in every single one of your videos makes complete and total sense. Let people know that you've got more for them to see by linking to playlists and linking to other videos; all of these ideas are very strategic and very easily implemented. They don't know you; they don't know that you have this other video; so linking to those things can be incredibly powerful.

When I write about "making sense" in annotations, I am talking about the simple fact that not all systems are going to support such annotations. Nothing is sillier than watching a video on a television set that says "click on the balloon" that isn't there or listening to video tell you that something is there, when, in fact, it isn't.

The first options "make sense" because they work regardless of whether the user can see them or not. An annotation that tells someone to subscribe is gold for someone who can see it, and it means nothing to someone who cannot.

All is not lost if all of your audience can't view your annotations. If you're linked to something external, address the fact that it might not work on their particular screen and give them an alternative. For example, you might have the video say "To learn more, go ahead and click on the link that says learn more and we'll take you right to an account over at Kickstarter. Or if you're viewing on a phone or a television set or other device which doesn't have external links, you can visit us at Kickstarter.com," then put that link right inside of the video file. Linking to something external and speaking about it is fine; you just need to address the fact that they might not be able to do that as well.

Finally, annotations asking people to give you a thumbs up are always doable. Of course, if you make it social, you get automatic sharing across all of the different networks. That is your best use of YouTube annotations.

I want to point out again that in the next chapter I examine what I consider to be the future of Annotations.

What Are YouTube Cards and Why Do They Matter?

It all started with YouTube Annotations. YouTube hoped to make their videos more interactive and developed a technology that worked quite nicely - on the computer desktop. There have to be millions of existing Annotations - if not billions.

But YouTube has changed. We watch more and more videos on our phones, tablets, and even TV sets. Consequently, the paradigm for interaction made possible with annotations simply doesn't "translate" technically and specifically to these new platforms.

YouTube describes Cards as the evolution of Annotations. I think the description fits. Cards are new, they can replace annotations, and they work in most of the places that Annotations didn't. They also provide some functionality that annotations never did. That's what I want to discuss here.

For the time being, both Annotations and Cards exist for YouTube producers and you are free to produce videos with both options.

You can see a great example of a Card in action here - https://www.youtube.com/watch?v=AskAQwOBvhc. It works on your phone and tablet as well as it does on your desktop.

Cards work a bit differently from Annotations. Instead of taking up the entirety of the screen to make the presentation, they offer a simple text overlay that, when clicked, triggers a more complete presentation either over the video (on the right hand side), or below the video (on many apps). This makes for a cleaner presentation - and this should leveraged in all of your YouTube Strategies . If you were wondering how long we'd be seeing videos where the talent points to an imaginary button and says "click here to buy" - that time has come.

At the time of writing there were six options for cards: Merchandise, Fundraising, Video, Playlist, Associated Website and Fan Funding. The purpose for each should be obvious and can really be used to extend the power of your video. In the example above, the video links directly to a book sales page, but the same feature could be easily integrated into all of these

It is important to point out that they aren't perfect; you don't really have an interface for Cards on the television set and some HTML5 players won't support them. So, like Annotations you should plan on them and use them, but don't them to make the video complete or you could alienate anyone who doesn't have access to the functionality.

Cards are new and the concept of interactive video is still a new concept to many - and we still have a number of years to go before this becomes common place. It is still a good idea to mention the Card if/when possible in the video to a) help the people who don't know what to do with it and b) speak to those who might not have access to it (i.e., a television viewer).

Because Cards are considerably "cleaner," you'll want to think through how you use them in your marketing efforts as they don't have to be as forceful as Annotations were. On the other hand, you don't want to make every single video you produce be a call to action, as part of the enjoyment of video is the ability to sit back and watch without requiring anything from the audience. What's the perfect balance? That's still to be determined - and is obviously different for every audience.

How do you add a card to your YouTube video? When you click to "Edit" a video in YouTube, the option pops up in the top menu bar. You then click "Add Card," pick the Card type and follow through on the rest of the prompts.

Can you put more than one Card on any given video? Yes, but don't overwhelm your audience and, strategically speaking, if your video has more than one call to action, you might want to consider splitting it into two different videos.

What is the future of Cards? It's impossible to tell at this point. Obviously, YouTube has the ability to kill them or change them, but they seem pretty set on this new option and they work quite nicely. I certainly see the addition of new Card options coming in the near to immediate future. If you register your copy of this book (see the About This Book section), we'll keep you up to date with any changes we hear of.

Because Cards are so powerful, I'm sure you're asking yourself what the future of Annotations is (and if you need to go back and change any of your previous work.) In their Creator Blog (http://YouTubeCreator.BlogSpot.com), YouTube stated that "our goal is to have these eventually replace annotations" but gave no specific date for the death of Annotations. As this point, I'm not convinced they'll wipe previous Annotations from the system but I can see, very soon, a time when you are no longer able to produce new ones.

What is the Best Format for a YouTube Video?

I never would have guessed how controversial my first response to this question would be. If you have a chance, visit this YouTube Video:

http://youtu.be/xR2TOwMmm2M

It has more than 70 thousand views (using the SEO techniques I write about in this book), coming almost entirely by Google Search (at the time of writing, it's the number one search result for almost every phrase possible that you can think of for this video) and has nearly five times as many thumbs down as thumbs up. If you really want an education on YouTube comments, take a look at what's there. It should scare you how much some people hate this video. That social stuff I mentioned earlier in this book? Almost daily I'm seeing posts of people saying how awful this video is and more. It's almost humorous.

As a side note though, this video is a perfect example of what happens when you do the kinds of things I write about in this book. Although it was published more than 2 years ago, it's seen nearly 500 views in the last week and the numbers keep going up. It has an annotation that is sending many people to my opt-in list and I couldn't be more thrilled with the results. Heck, I've even seen more than a hundred bucks in ads running on the thing. Not bad for a screencast-only video edited by my (then) 12 year old daughter.

Why the anger? What is their problem with the video? Am I, in fact, an idiot?

I get asked this question on a regular basis because it represents a big problem. When people are looking at making videos for YouTube, they often are faced with options of file formats of which they've never heard, especially if they're not using a Mac. Some video cameras have proprietary video formats that people don't recognize. In addition, if they've attended a class, or read a book or article by someone more interested in their business than education, they often get confused with buzzwords thrown around in an attempt to get more business.

In short, the beauty of YouTube is that it doesn't need to be that complicated. YouTube has spent an incredible amount of time and effort making it possible for you to upload your content without having to worry about the "nerdy" stuff. In short, the chances are good that if it's a valid video file format, YouTube will take it.

This allows you to focus on the content, not the technical stuff.

So why was my first response to this question so upsetting to so many? If you read the comments, a few have found some obscure file formats that YouTube doesn't accept (although I haven't been able to recreate any of their problems) and, if you notice carefully, many of them are more interested in the "fastest" versus the "best." A high quality video in HD (or more), as described a few chapters back is going to take some time. Take that time, it's worth it.

In short, YouTube takes any format you send them, so don't worry about it. Do they take X? Yes. Do they take Y? Yes. Do they take Mac? Linux? Windows? Yes, yes, and yes.

YouTube will take any video format produced by any major, realistic video editing system. So don't worry about transcoding or formatting for YouTube, just give them what you've got and let them take it from there. They will do everything they can to make it look as good as possible.

On the other hand, if you send them a dead duck, it's still a dead duck; regardless of whether or not it might be one of the best looking dead ducks they've ever had. Send them high quality, send them whatever format you want, and YouTube will make it look as good as possible.

It's part of what makes YouTube so cool: you don't have to worry about the format, bitrates, codecs and all these things you may have heard of or even worried about.

I did a live production and event where we did all the promotion across YouTube and saw tens of thousands of views on YouTube over the course of a week. Looking at the statistics and analytics for our whole program, we saw that there were hundreds of phone types that we didn't even know existed - we could only find about half of them on the internet with specs in English. People consume content from all over the world; and the great thing was that phones that I didn't know existed, with media players that I had never heard of, were consuming the content coming from YouTube.

That's the power of YouTube.

The great thing is, because they'll take any format, you can just send it to them and then breathe a sigh of relief. Keep your focus on the content instead.

The action items are simple. Focus on the content, not the format, and send the best quality video that you can.

For what it's worth, at the time of writing, YouTube officially claims support for the following formats:

1. .MOV

2. .MPEG4

3. .AVI

4. .WMV

5. .MPEGPS

6. .FLV

7. .3GPP

8. .WebM

I've seen them support others, but again, it's all about the content, not the format.

How to Script a YouTube Video That Brings Hungry Online Buyers Straight to You - By Gideon Shalwick

You might a lot of great people in this industry. Sometimes they're wicked smart. Sometimes they're great implementers. Sometimes they're a wonderful combination of both. Gideon is one of those wonderful implementers and his company Veeroll is one of the coolest "secret weapons" I've seen in a long time. Gideon scripts amazing YouTube ads and I asked him to give us his secrets. This chapter alone is worth the price of this book.

Foreword

Imagine for a second what your business would be like if you were able to use the EXACT right words in your ads that would instantly appeal to your target audience and get them to take massive action?

Trust me... if you know how to influence people with words, you are a LONG way there toward getting what you want out of life and out of business.

Recently, I ran a quick ad to one of my businesses using Veeroll. The script took me about 5-10 minutes to write... and in the end, we managed to get more clicks than views for the campaign!

Of course, I did have some good targeting in place for the ad, but without a great video script, my video certainly would not have produced so many clicks. But imagine how awesome it would be for you to pump out amazing video script after another, and get amazing results for your own campaigns too!

Since we started Veeroll, we noticed that one of the hardest things for our members to get right was the script for their video ads. Hence, I decided to write this little course on how to write effective scripts for video ads.

It's a crash course in helping you create better scripts for video ads whether you're using them on YouTube, Facebook or any other platform for that matter. But not only that, it will also help you with creating much better marketing messages for your business overall.

Once you know the formula, you can pump out amazing scripts one after the other, and improve the effectiveness of your video ads by orders of magnitude... and massively increase the number of clicks you get on your ads.

Words are powerful.

It can start wars. It can end wars. It can even send a man to the moon! In our case though, we just want to create awesome video ads :)

The more compelling your script, the more likely people will take action after watching your video! And that's exactly what we'll help you do with this report...

Ok, let's get into it...

Gideon Shalwick

Co-Founder, Veeroll

http://PaulColligan.com/Veeroll

Where To Start...

Introduction

Writing video scripts can be extremely rewarding (both personally and financially) when you get them right. Get them wrong though, and it may all seem like a big fat waste of time!

But where do you even start if you've never done anything like this before?

If you wanted to, you could just start with the formula I'll be explaining inside this report. In fact, here it is...

AIDCA

... which is short for Attention, Interest, Desire, Conviction and Action.

If you already understand what each of the 5 ingredients means, you could probably already create a pretty good video script.

But this report is not about creating pretty good scripts.

It's about creating ABSOLUTELY EXCELLENT video scripts to help you finally get the traffic you deserve for your business!

In the right hands, the above little formula could truly lift the effectiveness of your video ad scripts to heights you've never seen before!

But there's some leg work to be done before that little video script formula can help you get the clicks from your target audience.

There are 7 easy steps to follow that will help you create the BEST video ad scripts you'll ever create. Here they are...

Step 1: Define Your Target Audience

Step 2: Get Clear On The Problem Of Your Target Audience

Step 3: Find Out What Videos They Are Watching

Step 4: Define Your Solution That Solves This Same Problem

Step 5: Get Clear On The Unique Selling Proposition Of Your Solution

Step 6: Define Where You Want To Send Traffic

Step 7: Write The Script For Your Video Ad

It's only at step 7 that you'll need the little video script formula mentioned earlier. The steps before that will help you INCREDIBLY to create a much more powerful script for your video ad.

Ok, let's now get into each of the above 7 steps, and show you how fast and easy you can create these powerful little video ad scripts in no time!

Step 1: Define Your Target Audience

The very first question you should ask when creating a new video ad is...

WHO?

That is... WHO EXACTLY will you be targeting for your video ad?

This question drives EVERYTHING else for helping you create compelling video ad scripts. Get this wrong, and nothing else really matters.

The better you can know and understand your target audience, the easier it will be for you to go through the rest of the steps.

It pays in "interest" to spend more time on this first step to make sure you're crystal clear on who it is you want to target.

Common questions to help you figure out who your target audience is exactly, include...

- What kind of person is it?

- Is it a business person in a particular industry?

- Is it a non-business person in a particular niche?

- Are they male or female?

- Where do they live?

- What language do they speak?

- What kind of conversation is already going on their head?

- What kind of income do they have?

- What are their online habits?

- What kind of friends do they have?

Etc...

For some campaigns you'll need to do more research than others to get a very clear understanding of who you're trying to target.

All right... once you're clear on who you're targeting for your campaign, we're ready to move onto the next step...

Step 2: Get Clear On The Problem Of Your Target Audience

Next up, get clear on what exactly the problem your target audience is experiencing right now, that you can help them solve.

Of course this needs to relate back to your product or service that will eventually be the solution to their problem. But for now, think from the point of view of your target audience (the kind of person you defined in step 1). How might they describe the problem they are having to their best friend?

To help you get in the shoes of your target audience... image them lying in bed at night, thinking about this really annoying and painful problem that they are trying to solve.

This problem is so bad, they can't actually get to sleep - it's constantly eating away at them, and they wish they could find an instant solution to this really annoying and painful problem.

They might even be dreaming about having a magic wand they could just use to instantly get rid of this ugly problem!

You may find that there are multiple problems that your business or product or service may be able to solve for the same group of people. List them all here, and then prioritise them in the order of greatest problem, to smallest problem (from the point of view of your target audience of course!).

This step is another CRUCIAL step to make sure you create an effective video ad script. Step 1 helps you find the RIGHT PEOPLE to target. While Step 2 helps you find the RIGHT PROBLEM to solve for these people. Get any of these two wrong, and nothing else will help you improve the effectiveness of your ads!

If you can get these two first steps right, you've done most of the hard work, and you're about 80% towards creating a very compelling video ad that WILL convert!

Let's move on...

Step 3: Find Out What Videos Your Target Audience Is Watching

Next up, once you know who you're targeting, and what problem they're trying to solve, you need to figure out (roughly) what your target audience may be searching for on YouTube to try and solve this very same problem.

Knowing what kind of videos people are searching on for YouTube will put you in the right frame of mind to be able to write a video script that will be super relevant to your target audience.

Once again, put yourself in the shoes of someone in your target audience, and imagine what they might type into the YouTube search box to find a solution to their problem.

There's no need to get too exact here. And don't worry if you can't get it quite right at first - using the Keyword Search tool inside the Veeroll platform will certainly help you clarify EXACTLY what people are already searching for.

But for now, if you can just figure out what keywords you think people would use to find a video on YouTube that helps them solve their specific problem, it will help a lot!

Step 4: Define Your Solution That Solves This Same Problem

Now you're ready to bring your product or service (your solution) into the mix. But be careful here though. You don't actually want to describe your product or service for this part.

Instead, describe the solution that your product or service delivers to your target customer... and talk in terms of emotional benefits that your solution brings to your customers. Not just features.

See the difference?

One is from YOUR point of view... and the other is from the point of view of your target audience. It's a CRUCIAL distinction!

Step 5: Get Clear On Your Unique Selling Proposition

Defining your solution in terms that will appeal to your target audience is one thing, but it's not quite enough... especially in such a crowded marketplace where it's very common to have other similar products and services available to your target market.

So to help you stand out, you need a unique angle. Or more specifically, a Unique Selling Proposition (USP)!

For this part, figure out what makes your solution special or unique... especially from the point of view of your customer (not your point of view)!

Your USP will come in handy later when you start using the formula... so make sure you get crystal clear on this part as well before moving on...

Step 6: Define Where You Want To Send Traffic

This is the easiest part of the whole process - simply list where you'd like to send your traffic. This will be used later for the final line of your video ad script - the call to action (CTA).

You could send people to any page, as long as it's Adwords compliant of course. For example, you could send people to any of these...

- A YouTube video...
- A YouTube channel...
- A sales page...
- A squeeze page...
- A Facebook page...

...you get the idea!

Step 7: Write The Script For Your Video Ad

Finally, you're ready to start writing your script!

If you did a good job with the first 6 steps, this part should come very easy and natural for you.

Let's first look at the formula...

The formula is based on the age old selling formal of AIDCA (Attention, Interest, Desire, Conviction, Action). I've modified it slightly so it fits in better with the nature and structure of video ads.

Each part of the formula should take no longer than 5 seconds to convey your message. And in fact, that's exactly how we've setup the templates inside our Veeroll platform too!

Here is the formula again...

- Attention

- Interest

- Desire

- Conviction

- Action

Let's go into more detail now as each of these apply to video ads specifically. As you go through the formula, keep in mind the information you will have already gathered in the previous 6 steps. They are designed to help you figure out exactly what to use for each part of the formula.

Attention: Grab Their Attention In The First 5 Seconds

One of the best ways to grab people's attention in the first 5 seconds of your video, is to hone in on the exact pain point or problem that your target audience is experiencing.

When you get this right, you'll have what is known as "Audience To Problem Match". In other words... you will have targeted the THE RIGHT AUDIENCE, and you will have identified THE RIGHT PROBLEM that they are truly struggling with.

When you get a true "Audience To Problem Match", you'll have a MUCH higher chance of people watching past the first five seconds instead of clicking on the "skip" button in the case of YouTube In Stream Ads.

An easy way to tell whether you got this right, is to look at the watch time graph of your video. In general, ads normally have a sharp drop off after the first five seconds. But you should be able to reduce the drop off when you get true "Audience To Problem Match"!

Interest: Build Interest By Hinting At Your Solution

Once you've got the attention of your viewer, your next challenge is to KEEP their attention!

One of the best ways we've found to achieve this, is to create a massive open loop, intrigue or interest!

Remember, you only have 5 seconds here again to get people engaged. The idea is to peak the interest of the viewer, and get them to WANT to watch the rest of your video ad... instead of clicking on that pesky "skip" button!

One way to do this, is to give people a "hint" about your amazing solution. What you're looking to achieve here, is to get what's known as "Problem To Solution Match".

In other words, getting your viewer to realise that you actually have a practical solution to their exact problem. You need to make sure you are targeting THE RIGHT PROBLEM to solve, and secondly, that you have THE RIGHT SOLUTION to completely solve this problem.

This part is probably the hardest to get right from a script writing perspective. But you'll see how it works during our example soon...

The bottom line, is that you want to keep people's attention by drawing them into the rest of your video ad, and create a mental state in your viewer to WANT to completely watch the whole video ad!

Desire: Create Desire By Selling The Main Benefit Of Your Solution

For the next five seconds, your job is to "sell" your solution a bit more using the main benefit of your product. You need to convince your viewer WHY your solution is so amazing compared to everything else out there.

This is where your Unique Selling Proposition (USP) comes in.

With one simple statement about your USP, you can get people excited about your solution and positioning your solution (and the ONLY solution) to their specific problem.

Conviction: Apply A Psychological Trigger

Next, apply a powerful psychological "Trigger" to get people ready to take action during the CTA at the end. This is based on the 6 psychological "triggers" that Dr Robert Cialdini talks about in his amazing book "Influence". It's MUST READ recommended reading by the way!!!

Cialdini talks about 6 triggers to influence people to take action. These are:

1. Reciprocity

2. Commitment (and Consistency)

3. Social Proof

4. Liking

5. Authority

6. Scarcity

Out of these 6, I normally use Social Proof and Scarcity the most. Since you only have 5 seconds, you can only select one of these for your ad.

Let's quickly go through each of these to make sure you understand how to use them for your video ad script...

1. Reciprocity

The "Law Of Reciprocity" kicks in whenever something is given to someone else unexpectedly. The receiving person then feels "obliged" to "reciprocate"... that is, to want to give something back in return.

Often, sales people take advantage of this law, and might buy you a coffee or a meal while presenting their pitch to you. If they're paying for your meal, you may feel some obligation to at least listen, and even accept their proposal - even if you're not all that interested in it!

The way you can use it for your video ad script, is to mention something for free that you're giving away. Like a report, a video, some software... or whatever you think will appeal to your target audience.

So, it's not quite fully using the law of reciprocity, because technically the free gift has to be given first before the law kicks in.

But for the purpose of these video ad scripts, this will do :)

2. Commitment (and Consistency)

This is an interesting one...

The premise is that people normally act consistently with whatever commitments they've made.

For example, when you commit to a certain cause by signing a petition, you are so much more likely to take actions in support of that cause as well!

Sales people often use this by getting you to say "yes" to a range of smaller commitments, before asking you to take action on a much bigger commitment.

The way to use it for your video ad script, is to look for things that people in your target audience have already committed to, and then mentioning that and using that in your video script to get them to take a "consistent action" by clicking on your ad in the next part of the script... the call to action!

3. Social Proof

Personally, social proof is my second favourite out of all 6 triggers. The premise here is that, in general, people first want to see whether their peers have taken action before they take action on a particular thing as well. Sub-consciously, most people believe that there is safety in numbers. And therefore look for proof of that first before they take action.

There are at least 2 ways in which you can use the social proof trigger...

1. By mentioning the number of other people who have already taken action - the higher the number, the better of course!

2. Or by simply using a testimonial from one of your customers that represent your target audience.

3. Both of these can work amazingly well for getting people to take action at the end of your ad!

4. Liking

As you know, people like doing business with other people they LIKE, know and trust. That's what this trigger is all about. If you can get your target audience to instantly LIKE you... you've gone a long way to get them to take action on your video ad.

I find this one the hardest to use though, because you have so little time to build a relationship with your audience. 20-30 is hardly enough to get anyone to like you all that much really!

I haven't tried it yet, but you could try using humour quite effectively for "triggering" people to like you, or to grow some kind of affinity with your video ad.

But humour can also be very tricky to get right. So unless you really ARE good with humour, I suggest you don't try it! Or if you do try it, start with a smaller test first :)

Luckily there are two more triggers to choose from...

5. Authority

People naturally trust other people in a position of authority. Or even if they don't trust that person in authority, they may still do what they're being told to do by the authority!

Many fascinating psychological experiments have been run to prove this (actually on all the triggers, but I found the experiments for this one most interesting!).

If you're interested in more depth for this, I recommend you get yourself a copy of Robert Cialdini's Influence!

The way you can use this inside your video ad, is to get some kind of an endorsement from a recognised authority, expert or celebrity in your area of business. This would activate the "Authority" trigger and move people to action during your call to action without any trouble.

6. Scarcity

Finally, my favourite trigger! And the reason that it's my favourite is because it works so well!

Out of ALL the triggers, I've seen the "Scarcity" trigger perform the best.

The scarcity trigger gets activated as soon as there is a perceived lack of a wanted resource.

For example, think back to whenever you had to meet an important deadline. As you approached the deadline, and the remaining time became more "scarce", you probably noticed that you were taking more ACTION to meet the deadline.

Scarcity comes in many forms of course...

- Time
- Resources
- Product units available
- Spots available in a training course
- Etc

The key thing is that it's a wanted or desired, but limited, resource as perceived by your target audience.

The way to use it inside your video ad script, is to briefly mention any limit or lack related to your offer, and that people will be missing out unless they take action immediately.

Of course, please do NOT falsely manufacture scarcity (or any of the other triggers) - that will ALWAYS backfire back to you in some way!

- - -

All right... those are all 6 of the triggers. As I said earlier, I mostly use the social proof or scarcity triggers inside my video ad scripts, and the work VERY effectively.

Alternatively, if it does not make sense for you to use a trigger inside you video ad script, feel free to to extend on your USP or mention another strong benefit of your solution for this part.

In a moment I will show you the script for an ad that got a 144% click through rate. Part of it was getting the targeting right. But the other part was getting the script JUST right!

Let's move onto the final part of the formula...

Action: Call Your Viewer To Action

Finally... the only thing left is to call your viewers to take a specific action. This is by FAR the easiest part of the script.

Your aim for this part, is to simply ask people to click on your video... or on a certain part of your video. Adwords sometimes changes how their ads work, but use your creativity here to figure the exact call to action that is needed to help you get the best results for YouTube video ads and video ads from other platforms such as Facebook.

That's it!

If you've done a good job with the other parts of the formula, people will naturally WANT to take action. And all you have to do, is tell them what to do!

Let's now have a look at a quick example, to show you how fast and easy you can create these little video scripts...

A Detailed Case Study

For our example, let's have a look at one of my other businesses that I recently ran an ad for... Splasheo.com.

Please note that at the time of writing this, Adwords still had things setup to have the WHOLE video clickable. Recent news just came out that they will be changing how that works, and where people will be able to click. So please keep this in mind as you go through this example.

As some background, for this ad, I wanted to promote our flagship product, video intros - short animations of company and product logos that can be used inside people's videos to spice them up a bit.

This particular ad fetched a healthy 144% click through rate for some targeting groups (as measured as clicks over views), and managed to get me some extremely low cost traffic to my site.

Here are the steps I went through...

Step 1: Define Your Target Audience

Business owners who are currently editing their own videos. In other words, they do not use an external company to create and edit videos for them. They like doing it themselves either because of cost constraints or because they love the creativity of it.

These people are not professional video editors, but they are looking for an easy way to make their videos look great.

They are already looking for an intro online, but can't find a nice solution that looks professional enough and at the right price.

Step 2: Get Clear On The Problem Of Your Target Audience

They want their videos to look professional, but they can't afford to hire an expensive video editing team, and they don't have the expertise themselves to create something professional looking. They wish they could just wave a magic wand and magically make a beautiful video intro appear that they can then use inside their videos.

Step 3: Find Out What Videos They Are Watching

They are watching videos related to "video intro animations" or just "video intros". And they are searching for either free solutions, or simple software that can help them create professional looking intros fast and easy and at a cost they can afford.

Terms they might use when searching for this on YouTube include:

- video intro
- video intro tutorial
- video intro software
- logo animation
- logo animation software
- etc

Step 4: Define Your Solution That Solves This Same Problem

Get a professional video intro created for you. All you have to do, is select from a range of templates, and then upload your logo, and then everything else gets done for you.

Step 5: Get Clear On The Unique Selling Proposition

No video editing required, whatsoever!

Step 6: Define Where You Want To Send Traffic

To the product page for Splasheo. In this case it's www.splasheo.com/products where people can make their selection and purchase their intro.

Step 7: Write The Script For Your Video Ad

And here is the script for this video ad...

- Attention: Need A New Intro For Your Video?

- Interest: There's A REALLY Easy Way To Do It Now...

- Desire: All You Need Is Your Logo Image...

- Conviction: The Rest Gets Taken Care Of For You...

- Action: Click The Button Now To Get Yours TODAY!

You can watch the video ad here to see what it came out as:

https://www.youtube.com/watch?v=ACDFPYneUsg

Note for this example, we followed the formula relatively closely. The main deviation was with the trigger. For this particular video ad, we decided not to use a trigger, but to instead expand on the USP of the product.

If we were running a limited time promotion, we might have modified the script by using a very strong scarcity trigger in the second last line. Like this...

- Attention: Need A New Intro For Your Video?

- Interest: There's A REALLY Easy Way To Do It Now...

- Desire: All You Need Is Your Logo Image...

- Conviction: 50% Discount For The Next 24 Hrs Only!

- Action: Click The Button Now To Get Yours TODAY!

BOOM!

How easy was that!

See how you can pump these out in no time?

You bet!

Final Thoughts...

That's the whole method, formula and case study in a nutshell!

Trust me when I say that MANY books have been written on this topic, and many, many courses have been created to help business owners get their messaging right.

What we've done here, is condensed a bunch of knowledge and honed it into writing 5 lines of text of 40 characters each. And the challenge is to do it so well, that people can't resit to click on your ad and visit your website!

In the Appendix, I've listed a few of the books I consider as MUST READ material if you're truly serious about creating SUPER effective video advertising.

But still the BEST way to learn, is through taking action and repetition. So, I recommend you go and create your first video ad script right away, get it created by Veeroll, then submit it Adwords, and see what happens.

The great thing with Veeroll is that you can create multiple video's all at once, and then run them together as a split test inside Adwords. And of course, for your testing, you don't have to spend much money with Adwords at all to see how effective your ads are.

This way, you can learn extremely fast about what works in your industry and what does not - and in no time become a total Video Ad Script Writing JEDI!!!

Now it's your turn.

I greatly look forward to seeing your amazing video ads totally CRUSH it on YouTube, and sending you endless amounts of awesomely qualified traffic that converts into sales.

Here's to your video ad success!

Gideon Shalwick

Co-Founder, Veeroll

http://PaulColligan.com/Veeroll

Recommended Reading

Here's a list of some INCREDIBLE books that will not only help you write better video scripts, but it will also help you become a MUCH better business person! Seriously, the following books are worth their weight in GOLD... and I would even say... priceless!

Get them. Read them. Become awesome. Nuff said.

- Influence - The Psychology Of Persuasion - by Robert Cialdini

- Breakthrough Advertising - by Eugene Schwartz

- Scientific Advertising - by Claude Hopkins

- Tested Advertising Methods - by John Caples

- Ogilvy On Advertising - by David Ogilvy

What Value is There in Closed Captioning your YouTube Videos?

A lot of people don't know that YouTube actually does automatic closed captioning. At this point in time, they provide it for English only; but that will probably change soon. It's done using the same technology that they utilize in the Google Voice product, which means, at least the time of writing, their automatic closed captioning is terrible.

So, yes, you can get closed captioning from YouTube, automatically, but it's really bad. I've actually considered dedicating a channel about the bad closed captioning that comes from Google and YouTube, because it's just so off, and wrong, and... funny. With the way this technology is going and the nuances of close captioning videos, I honestly don't see it improving for many years.

Now that the "they-do-it-for-free" angle has been dealt with, let's explore the topic with the focus it deserves.

YouTube does offer search results based on closed captioning content and they will show results accordingly. The implications of this should be thrilling for anyone looking to get their content viewed. Think about it: a 15-minute video might have a lot of words in it. But somebody searching for a certain term or phrase might find it in minute seven of that video. The good news is, YouTube will offer you the ability to go right to that part of the video within the search results. That capability is quite profound and shows how integrated YouTube and Google really are.

Also, realize that instead of just optimizing your video with the title, description, tags and links, you can actually optimize your video so that every single word said within the video also contains keywords. Scripting your video suddenly begins to make sense; and you can totally use this to your advantage.

What's interesting is that outside of searching, there are actually some additional advantages to optimizing your video's closed captioning. You should realize that there is a tremendous audience of people who can't hear or are unable to consume audio for one reason or another. If you have close captioning for your videos, you have suddenly given that demographic the ability to consume your content. It's still a very under-served audience and they'll appreciate the opportunity you've given them.

What's also important is that there are a number of people who want to watch videos without disturbing others; whether they are at work, on a bus, or on some sort of transport where having their audio go out loud might get them into trouble. The bottom line: if you've got close captioning you might get video consumption that you wouldn't get otherwise.

At this point Google does not provide search facilities through the transcripts. But... we know it's coming. Google owns YouTube, YouTube searches the transcripts... why in the world wouldn't they tie those two together? So, although at this point Google doesn't search the transcripts, logically, it has to be coming soon.

Finally, if you do put together a transcript for your video, not only can you upload it to YouTube but you can also put that content up on your blog. Now, every word that you produced becomes searchable by Google.

In the best case scenario, you should get all your videos

transcribed and upload the transcripts for each video. At this point, people always want to know a good transcription company; I will make sure we have a good one listed for you in the "Additional Resources" chapter of this book.

If you can't do that, at least edit the automatically-generated text within the closed captioning, and make sure that it captures your most important keywords correctly. If you do that, you'll get a slight bump – nothing like what you get with full transcripts – but a bump none-the-less. At the top of the list of quick corrections, you will want to make sure all brand and proper names are spelled correctly. You'd be surprised how many different ways YouTube has tried to spell "Colligan."

Shooting Videos that Sell - By Travis Shields

Travis Shields is my favored video guy and has done some amazing work for some pretty amazing people. He's an award-winning filmmaker with over 15 years of professional video production experience. For the past five years he has produced lucrative video campaigns for top internet marketer, Brendon Burchard. I've asked him to write a few words about shooting videos that sell.

These days, most of us have at least one video camera, if not more. We have camcorders; webcams; we even have cameras on our cell phones. And the editing tools are plentiful too. Free or inexpensive editing software like iMovie (Mac) and Windows Movie Maker (PC) are standard apps on our computer. But even with all these tools available now, creating great video has long been seen as a very complicated, expensive and challenging process.

Of course, the best way to make sure you have the best quality possible on your videos is to hire a pro. But with budgets being what they are, it's not always feasible to hire a videographer every time you need to shoot something.

People often ask me what camera they should buy or what is the latest editing software out there. While that's all important info, the most important thing to understand is that you need to pick up whatever camera nearest to you and GET STARTED. Online video is the fastest way to convey your message, reach the largest audience and sell your product or program. That's why I created an online course (shameless self-promotion) called "Shoot Videos That Sell", which teaches how you can easily create good-looking videos no matter what your budget is.

In this bonus chapter I want to focus less on HOW you're going to shoot your videos and more on WHAT your videos should be about.

Step 1. Define the goal of your video.

What is the goal of your video? Is it to promote your brand? Get people to buy, sign up, donate or subscribe? If so, who do you want your message to get to? These are the most important questions to answer, and they need to get answered before you hit the record button. People are looking to you for the fastest way to get from point A to point B. So give them what they want and shorten their learning curve. Remember: YOU are the expert.

Step 2. Create a video script or outline.

Get your ideas down on paper. Depending on your comfort level in front of the camera you may want to use a teleprompter (like I do) or at the very least bullet points to keep the flow of your video moving. Just make sure that if you are using a teleprompter that your voice doesn't sound like you are reading. Keep your energy level up and sound enthusiastic. I use a phrase with my clients called "Talking past the lens" which means projecting your voice past the camera. I like to visualize the viewer watching you at home in this tiny little video window on their computer. It's a small window, so you've got to project and be interesting or else the viewer will click away. Don't be afraid of that scary lens; make the camera your new best friend.

Step 3. Create a visual Bible.

What do I mean by that? A visual Bible is simply a list of visual ideas and concepts that you want to incorporate in your videos.

What do you want your video to look like? What's the look of your set or background going to be?

What is the feel and tone of your video? How do you want the audience to feel when they see your video? What kind of music will help convey this feeling? Keep working towards these ideas until you achieve them.

Step 4. Find an Emotional Connection

Figuring out how to wrap a story around what you're selling is critical to success in video. People want to know how you became an expert. Sharing your personal story of struggle and how you came up with the solution sets you up as the expert and creates trust. You've got to find that emotional connection.

Step 5. Clear Call-To-Action

A critical part of any video is to ensure a clear call-to-action.

Tell them what to do!

This could be a graphic at the end of the video that points people to a website for more information, provides a phone number, or lists an email address.

Make it really clear the action you want people to take.

At the very least make sure you are capturing their name and email address so you can start building your email list and have a growing audience to sell to later.

Step 6. Review/Reshoot

Look, nobody is perfect. Some of my videos I had to film three times before I was able to properly convey my message. So have your friends and family watch your video before you promote it and make sure that it makes sense and that it works.

It's easy to freeze up on camera and seem sort of stiff and rehearsed.

The only way to really overcome this is practice.

Don't be afraid of re-shooting something that isn't working. But at the same time, don't get too caught up in perfection so that you never finish the video.

If you mess up and it's funny, it's okay to roll with it; make fun of yourself and move on. It just shows that you are actually a real person and not a robot.

Step 7. Promote, Promote, Promote

YouTube, Facebook, Twitter, Instagram, email, word-of-mouth.

Do them all.

Build your email list and get your sales video in front of as many people as possible.

I hope these tips were helpful to you. I've been shooting video professionally for 15 years now and I know that having a game plan is important, but not as important as setting up your camera (hopefully on a tripod), pressing record, and getting started. TODAY.

————————————————

For a free video from Travis on how to shoot videos "exactly like Apple" (it's pretty impressive), visit http://PaulColligan.com/Shoot.

Do You Need a Camera to Make A Great YouTube Video?

This chapter will liberate some and frustrate others.

In short, the answer is no, ... you don't need a camera to make a great YouTube video. In fact, grabbing a camera, might be a really bad strategy.

Were not just talking about "faces made for radio" here - we're talking about video development strategies that, simply, don't require a camera.

What Are You Trying To Accomplish?

Part of a good YouTube Strategy is understanding the goal for your video. For some, the goal is something along the lines "putting a personal face on the company" or something else that obviously requires a camera. For others, the goal might not require a camera at all. Lets examine a few of these options and, possibly, take a heavy load off your shoulders.

The Screencast Video

One of my most successful YouTube videos is an hour-plus recording of a Webinar I did with an associate on the topic of Facebook Marketing. The Webinar sold a training program (that no longer is available) and made me thousands of dollars in affiliate revenue. In addition, by letting YouTube monetize the video with ads, I brought in hundreds of additional dollars from advertising. The video added hundreds of subscribers to my Channel and account for more than a half a million minutes of viewing time.

By the way, you can view that video here - https://www.youtube.com/watch?v=9VfXljgensI

I need to stress - no cameras were used in this video - it was the recording of a Webinar using nothing but PowerPoint Slides and commentary by myself and my associate.

Screencasting is a viable option for YouTube videos - don't leave the option out of your YouTube Strategies .

You can record your computer screen using a program called "Screenflow" for the Mac (look it up in App Store) and "Camtasia" for Windows machines.

The Animation Video

There are number of tools that will create gorgeous animation videos from pre-designed template that you personalize for your own needs and requirements.

The video found here - http://www.youtube.com/watch?v=nd7iqAAIxhM - was made my (at the time) 12 year old daughter in less than an hour.

How did she do it? She used the program VideoMaker FX - which can be found at http://PaulColligan.com/VFX

What does the program do? I made this short video using the program to explain - http://www.youtube.com/watch?v=SeY2I0vCzX8

VideoMaker FX isn't the only program out there that makes animation videos - but it sure is easy enough for me to use (and at a price that I don't mind spending).

I find animation videos such as these to be as effective as producing a more traditional video - and you might just find the same.

The Outsourced Video

Finally, remember that just because HD Cameras are inexpensive and plentiful doesn't mean you're a videographer (or should be one) any more than a cheap spatula at the Dollar Store can make you a chef.

Sometimes outsourcing your video is the smartest video production move you can make

Consider outsourcing your video. From viable $5 options found at Fiverr (http://PaulColligan.com/Fiverr - discussed elsewhere in this book) to the hiring of a professional crew, you might just find that the camera needed to make your video might not be your camera at all.

Why the "Wrong" Music for YouTube Videos Can Cause a Lot Of Problems - and How To Prevent Them - By Mike Stewart

The first album I bought as a kid was "Pac Man Fever" (yes, I've been computer guy since pretty much day one) and Mike Stewart played keyboards on that Gold Record "back in the day." We've been friends since the day we've met (long before I learned of Pac Man Fever connection) and I've respected his ability to create fun music and making some of the most complicated issues simple.

My name is Mike Stewart and I have been marketing online as the "Internet AudioVideo Guy" since 2001 because audio and video are my passions in business. I started out composing music for advertising, corporations, and even national broadcast TV back in 1979. Even from the beginning, professional video producers have been keen on pairing the right music to underscore the message or visuals; the wrong music could ruin the effectiveness, comprehension and power of the piece. They also knew that if they did not have the sync rights to the music, they could be in violation of copyright, which would mean letters from lawyers or even lawsuits. Using popular music in videos, whether corporate or broadcast, required a sync license from the copyright owner or publisher. Years ago, we had a client who wanted to use "Bye Bye Love," a song written by Felice and Boudleaux Bryant in a commercial for pet flea collars, changing it to "Bye, Bye Fleas". Creative - right? At least so they thought. The publishers wanted $80,000 in 1985 for a 1 year license; a number which caused the client to nearly choke. They opted for us to compose something original for a lot less money, not because they wanted that, but because they knew they had to stay legal and match the music to the video. Our tune did the job and they didn't have any legal issues.

Back in those days, the pipe to deliver video content was shipping tapes, TV tower transmitters and satellites. All of those systems were totally beyond the reach of individuals and small businesses because of cost and corporate control. Fast forward to 2004 and the advent of broadband internet connections and streaming video starting that really worked and the pipe changed. Better yet, everyone was welcome to use it for free! Finally, making video content and broadcasting it to the world was possible for everyone, not just corporations

I personally was never more excited! I worked in the days when making video content professionally required one hundred thousand dollars or more of equipment and skills only professionals knew. This was back in the day that only the select few with the budgets to produce and distribute could get content broadcast. Personal computers, tablets, cheap editing software, HD cameras in your phone, and the internet, especially YouTube, changed all that. Now, if you can produce content, you can reach the world with your content.

What has not changed is copyright laws, and the skill to pair the right music to the right scene.

Now that everyone has a pipe to distribute video content, what problems must be avoided?

1. Always use music you have the rights to use, with a license from the music producer proving you are royalty free. YouTube has made publishers prove this by requiring them to send proof of license. If they

didn't, videos were deleted and channels were erased.

2. Be objective to be certain that the feel of the music complements the visual and message. Royalty free music libraries group tracks in tempos, moods, and emotions. A problem arises when the feeling from the music underscoring doesn't match the message.

3. Make sure music comes in and out, and is not too loud to cover narration. Sometimes constant music works, but more times than not, silence is a great emphasis that punctuates the entrance of a new theme.

4. Just because you see a lot of copyrighted music on YouTube, don't think it makes it legal. The music publishing industry is not able to police all the infringements. They seem to turn a blind eye when it is a fan just loving the music, but if you use music for commercial promotion, then they can come after you for infringement. When making business videos, be legal.

Streaming video in all its delivery options, like YouTube, Vimeo, Wordpress, and MP4/HTML5 players, is here to stay. The pipeline is open to everyone and the reach is now the world. I was lucky enough in 1980 to meet Ted Turner here in Atlanta and hear him say, "I can reach 7.5 million homes with my TV station WTBS." That didn't mean they were watching, it meant that 7.5 million people had access to his content, and that was a big deal; in fact it was the inspiration for launching CNN. You have access to over 3.5 billion viewers with your content, but like Ted, you have to create great content, spend time and money marketing to get viewers, and stay legal with the copyrights you use. For video content, it has always been the law. If you didn't create it, you must have permission or you will open yourself to problems.

Don't let this problem happen to your videos!

If you pick music that confuses the viewer, the goal of your message can and will be lost.

The most exciting broadcast days of television are yet to come, and you are a part of it. I know I will be participating myself from now on. I wish that for you as well.

Mike Stewart

http://LegalPodcastMusic.com

p.s., Mike's site - LegalPodcastMusic.com offers an amazing price on a huge collection of audio that you can integrate into all of you YouTube Videos (Podcasts too!) without any of the legal worries Mike writes about above.

What Quality Should I Publish my YouTube Videos in?

There are a lot of people who love to get techy, nerdy and distracted with their videos' optimum bit-rate and functional rate. In spite of all that, it's really simple: YouTube will take whatever it can possibly get and will do everything it can to make it look as awesome as possible.

They've got brilliant people who have been put on this task. So, YouTube can handle better quality than you could have possibly seen anywhere. Just publish at the best possible quality and they'll do the work with everything else. YouTube can dumb it down for people with slow computers, phones with small screens, etc. Just send whatever you've got in the highest possible quality.

What about format...X? Format X works great. YouTube takes it all, that's part of the beauty of what YouTube does.

Also remember that when you post a YouTube video, this content is going to be online for years. If you do it right, you can produce a video that has a shelf life of four, six, seven, even ten years. Giving them a low quality video might be possible right now, but what's going to happen in ten years?

I write at the end of this book of 4K video, what others might call Ultra HD. You probably don't have the capacity to make those kinds of videos yet, but you should be aware that YouTube is ready to take those as well. They are thinking far into the future and you should too.

Over time, YouTube is extremely powerful; so you want to do everything you can to upload the video that doesn't just look good now, but that looks good as far into the future as possible. And again, realize that YouTube does all the downgrading and all the cross-grading, so you don't have to worry about that.

Action item number one (really the only one) is to publish all videos at the best possible quality you can. The majority of videos right now are uploaded to YouTube in 1080p quality. Make it your goal to send video that is at least that quality or, if possible, even better.

Yes, it takes additional disk space and processing power to generate, edit and store video of this quality but it will be worth it in the long run.

If you own a powerful editing system and you've got a video editing station that can produce even higher than 1080P, go ahead and send them that; YouTube can handle it and it will last longer for you down the road.

Do remember that some people are watching videos on mobile phone screens. Although you are sending YouTube a massive file – one that shows the flies on the back of the horses as they are running through the fields in crystal clarity – not everybody will be able to watch in that sort of definition. Send the high quality video, but develop a video that still looks good if viewed on a screen that's no bigger than a couple of square inches.

So again, publish all the videos at the best possible quality you can: 720 at the bare minimum, and 1080 if at all possible. If you could do even better, absolutely do it. But then, despite all the quality, remember that some people are consuming videos on small screens with slow connectivity; so plan your content accordingly.

In the "What's Next at YouTube" chapter I speak about Ultra

HD and what YouTube is doing with it. It might be worth your time to take a peek at that chapter if this is at all an option to you.

How Do I Get my Videos to Link Outside of YouTube?

YouTube doesn't make it easy to link your videos outside of YouTube because of the damage that could come from this. Think about it; anybody can upload to YouTube, and they can upload anything they want and link it to anything they want. If they endorse a website that sends people to a malware site or sends people to spyware, the amount of damage that could be done quickly is something that YouTube has to be incredibly cautious about.

As a result, YouTube doesn't make this easy because of the potential damage that could be caused. If you are playing the YouTube game, you need to understand this reality.

However, there are ways that anybody can achieve an external link - and it is well worth the effort. Here are your options.

Option one: just ask for the link inside of the video; you'd be surprised how easy this is and how well it works. Just say in your video, "Visit my website at www.x.com." If you also include some text saying "Visit my website at www.x.com," or wear a t-shirt or a hat with the URL, that works surprisingly well too (and translates fabulously across all devices). If you don't ask, you don't receive.

Again, you should realize you might have a video that YouTube allows you to provide an external link on. But if someone is watching on their phone or their Xbox, etc., they can't click on the link. So sometimes, it's about integrating the link into the video and asking people to visit the link within your content.

A second option is to include the exact link within your description. When you put the link inside of the description for your YouTube video, and you write it as http://www.x.com , YouTube will hyperlink that for you (for any device that supports it). In fact, there have been incredible results that have come from that. Again, be aware that people viewing from mobile devices or televisions might not have that opportunity; so don't make that the only place that you include the external link.

Option number three is to place ads on your video through http://Ads.YouTube.com ; but again, those only work with a system that supports that, so don't rely on that method entirely either.

Option number four is linking with an annotation link. Inside of an annotation link (remember again that this doesn't work on all platforms) you can link to other videos outside of YouTube, you can link to playlists inside of YouTube, to channels inside of YouTube, subscription options, or to a Google+ profile page. This works quite nicely to get people to playlists, channels and to Google+ profile pages.

At the time of writing YouTube also supports linking within annotations to "Fundraising Projects", "Associated Websites" and "Merch". These options are very exciting and should be considered. If links to "Associated Websites" are open to you, and you associate your website with your channel (currently available through the "Features" option under your "Channel Settings" menu), you have the ability to link DIRECTLY to any page within the site associated with your YouTube Channel. The implications of this should be obvious.

WIth that said and done, here are your action items:

Number one: do as many of these options as is possible. YouTube is nice, but, obviously, your site is nicer. Definitely make it part of the video and definitely make it part of the description. Make it part of the annotation if that makes sense but in addition to that, make it clear why you want them to leave. To just say "Visit my website for X," in reality won't work. Why? Because I'm on YouTube, I'm on my phone, on my X-box, on my Apple TV; whatever it is that I'm doing, I'm not going to leave to visit your website.

You have to make it very clear why you want them to leave. "Come here and I'm going to give you this" or "Come here and you're going to get that." Make it very clear why they need to do it now, as opposed to in the future. Give them a reason and you'll have a lot more chances for them to actually link to something outside of YouTube.

Finally, just address the possibility that not all devices will be equipped to show all of your content. You have annotations, you have ads, you have a bunch of things. You should say in the video, "Look, if you're watching this on your computer, there are 47 ways to visit my website or find out other things that I'm doing. But of course, if you're watching this on your phone, you don't have those options, so you might as well X." That makes complete sense; people enjoy it and people appreciate it. And that's how you get your videos to link outside of YouTube.

Look into the Associated Website option in your annotation link options. If you have access to that, certainly leverage it; but still apply all the rules mentioned above.

Finally, read the chapter on YouTube Cards as they give you some additional options for linking from your site that you might want to consider. Functionally, they are the same as annotations, but they work on mobile devices better and are, in my opinion, a considerably more attractive interface to work with.

How Can I Optimize my YouTube Channel and Videos? What About Mobile?

A considerable amount of YouTube video is being viewed on mobile devices; mostly over phones, although in many cases on tablets as well. Mobile is the fastest growing market for YouTube, as well as the fastest growing online market for pretty much everybody. Every batch of statistics point to the same fact: mobile is growing and you need to be part of it.

Last year YouTube introduced the "OneChannel" program (http://www.YouTube.com/OneChannel). The idea is simple. Because we're connecting to YouTube in so many different ways - phone, tablet, television, etc., we need a single channel format that supports all of these options. This was a smart strategy for YouTube - and it is a smart strategy for you.

Don't worry - part of the beauty of YouTube is that you don't have to do a anything (other than upload high-quality video) to get your content ready for the phone, the tablet or the television set. Not only does YouTube optimize the video for whatever screen the customer might be viewing, they also make sure they serve the best content for whatever bandwidth your customer is connecting with. This is why you can stream a video on your phone on the bus on the way to work and finish that video on a 52-inch television set at home.

You do have to take a couple of things into consideration when you think about video over so many platforms. Clicks, annotations and ads don't always work as well on mobile devices as they do on desktop computers or television sets. You need to optimize your Channel and videos with this reality in mind.

Many people think of YouTube only in the terms of the traditional YouTube page on the Web. Many use annotations, ads and descriptions under the videos because they are so powerful when viewed in the traditional desktop browser.

If you've watched any amount of YouTube video, you've probably seen people say "Click on the links below" or mention an annotation for something like subscribing to a Channel. If you're watching on a phone, you won't see links below. If you say something like "Click on this annotation," the mobile device interface may or may not show it. This can be very confusing for your (now extended) audience, which is not the experience they were looking for.

Since clicks, annotations and ads don't always work as well across all platforms, your task is to not say or do anything that will make you look bad. Don't call the annotations and links out as a matter of fact, because a lot of people, possibly the largest percentage of your audience, won't be able to view them or interact with them. Telling someone to "click on the links below" can actually have the opposite of the desired effect; instead of links being clicked, your audience may think that your video is simply broken.

OneChannel Strategies

Number one: realize that your videos might be viewed by someone with a two-inch screen or a 52-inch television (neither of which support any kind of clicks). For example, you may have done a screencast of a high-definition computer screen that you broadcast on YouTube (screencasting is a tremendously profitable element of YouTube, and it's growing in leaps and bounds.) If you have someone who is consuming your screencast on a two-inch screen, it may lose all of its effectiveness. If your video has small lettering and titles, or large sweeping vistas and really dramatic video shots, these won't come across on a two-inch screen either. At the same time, a video which looks good on television might lose everything when viewed on a phone.

Furthermore, you must realize that someone watching your content on a two-inch screen won't have the ability to interact with your video. What you want to do is to consider opt-in choices that don't require this level of interactivity.

For instance, instead of saying "Click to visit my website," you can say out loud, within your video, "Visit my website at www.x.com." Instead of saying "Send me your name and email address to get a report or to get a coupon," you might ask your viewer to text you his or her name and email address. There are platforms that make this both very possible and very profitable and I examine them in more detail in the "Paul's Favorite Tech" chapter of this book.

In short, whenever you add any call-to-action mechanisms to your video, just ask yourself: "Will this work for people in front of a computer? Will this work for people in front of a TV set? Will this work for people using a phone?"

Half Your Audience Is Mobile

At the time of writing, half of the YouTube audience is mobile. This number is only going to go up as more and more people find mobile connections to be faster and cheaper than ever before.

For every minute you examine your YouTube handiwork on the desktop, consider viewing your videos on your phone and you channel on both a mobile browser and the YouTube App on whatever mobile devices you have access to. It's a different world - but it's more than half your audience - so you need to understand how they view your channel as well and, more importantly and make channels if/when needed.

Live is Mobile Too

I examine the elements of broadcasting live to YouTube elsewhere in this book. It isn't always obvious that everything YouTube broadcasts (including live) is optimized for all screens; so when you are planning out your live events, remember your growing audience on the smartphone and television.

What Can I Do to Maximize my YouTube Channel?

Everybody wants to maximize their YouTube Channel—and you should make use of every tool you have to achieve this purpose. YouTube's OneChannel concept (http://www.YouTube.com/OneChannel) proves their commitment to making the experience as profitable and as efficient as possible for all of the different screen types that might be looking to access your content. Now, I am able to tell my audience, regardless of which device they are using, to visit my Channel at http://www.YouTube.com/Colligan and know that I can provide an optimal experience for all of them.

YouTube has more than a billion unique visitors a month. Don't you want access to that? The fact is that YouTube wants people to help them build the brand. If you build out your channel, you build out their brand; and as a result, they will like you more—which will be reflected in your rankings and your ratings in the search engine.

YouTube wants content creators to build their brand on YouTube. This is good for you and this is good for YouTube. These are the kind of win-wins that should be part of any and every strategy online. Even if you are building your brand elsewhere (as you should), make sure your brand-building efforts on your YouTube Channel get the time and attention they deserve.

How is this good for YouTube? When you send people to

your channel to find other videos, to find playlists or to interact with your channel, you're getting your audience to utilize the YouTube interface; which is exactly what YouTube wants.

YouTube wants users who help them build their brand. Why? Because the more people come to their site, the more they can charge for advertising. Consequently, the more you have built out your Channel, and the more interactivity it brings, the more YouTube will like you and appreciate you as a user.

When any audience member subscribes to your Channel, every time you put up a new video, they are alerted on the home page. This is actually how YouTube makes the majority of their money. So, when you create a video, it's a solid strategy to ask the viewer to subscribe to your channel. Then, when you put up a new video, the channel automatically updates and it brings people to your channel page.

In short, a channel optimized for all screens and a subscriber strategy to bring users back to YouTube, plus the additional content you provide, brings YouTube the very audience they are looking for. They'll return the favor with the very positioning and attention for your channel that you are looking for.

The Artwork

The artwork for your OneChannel is not formatted as most would think - and certainly not at all like the traditional social media graphics you see on other sites. As a result, there are a number of people who have "upgraded" to the OneChannel format and now have a graphic that looks great on one platform, but not all of the others. I've often pondered making a video of some of the mistakes of some very big brands... but I'd rather focus on doing things right.

The way your artwork is designed is best explained in visual form. Below is a great video from YouTube that shows you

exactly what you need to do for optimum results.
http://youtu.be/ES4-rTAB1L4

At the time of writing, YouTube recommends your art be 2560x1440 in size.

The Trailer Video

New to the OneChannel program is a trailer video; this is a video offered to people who visit your Channel but who are not yet subscribed. This is your chance to tell them why they should subscribe and to encourage them to do so. You'd be surprised how many don't know they can subscribe to a YouTube Channel and will be thrilled with the person who introduces them to the concept. Don't you want to have that special place in their heart?

Think long-term for your trailer video. The social impact of a trailer video with thousands of views says a lot more than a video changed on a regular basis (for whatever reason). Think about it; if you were looking at a YouTube Channel page that was asking you to subscribe and you saw the video only had 11 views, what would you think about that channel?

I think my trailer video at
http://www.YouTube.com/Colligan does a good job at this - and I don't see myself changing out the video any time soon. Note that I also use it to build a list external to the one I have at YouTube. This has proven very effective for me. Feel free to use it as a model for your own efforts.

Build A Channel Worth Subscribing To

First and foremost, build a channel worth subscribing to. Take some time to think through the process: get a solid piece of channel art; build playlists; collect links; write descriptions; and make a homepage that you can be proud of - and that people will actually want to subscribe to.

Secondly, always ask people to subscribe to your channel—

this one is huge. Many see YouTube as nothing more than a collection of videos and simply don't know that subscription is an option. When people subscribe to your channel, it builds your YouTube page and it's good for everybody involved.

If at all possible, build a trailer video that is designed for the long-term and encourages your audience to subscribe both on Youtube and through some external list-building mechanism.

What Should I Do After I Publish my YouTube Video?

What should you do after you publish your YouTube video to ensure you get the most views and traffic possible? Let's start with the simple fact that changes everything: YouTube weighs their rankings strongly based on how long people watch the video. This is not a theory; they've said this publicly time and time again.

At one time your strategy was to get as many views as possible for your video because it would result in the best ranking possible (along with the social proof that comes from a bunch of views). In short, you simply bought cheap views, from any source, and let math do the rest.

That path, thank goodness, is no longer effective. Your strategy, now, is to get as many people as possible to watch as much as possible of the video, and the entire video if possible.

Again, please don't do anything silly like buy views or get a bunch of people to click on the video and then leave. Speaking of math, if you get a couple of hundred people to view only four or five seconds of a four-minute video, you're now directly telling YouTube that people aren't finding what it is that this video had promised. Subsequently, you get pushed into a ghetto of sorts... and you don't want that.

Regarding this whole "math" thing, you just need to think the process through. Which is Google more likely to offer: a video that people watch until the end, or a video that people (and lots of them) watched for a few seconds and then left? Now that Google tracks these things, we need to change our strategies accordingly. So realize that they now weigh strongly on how long people watch the video, and never do anything silly like buying views or traffic.

What are your action items? How can you get high-quality views (as deep into the video as possible)?

Number one: when you publish a video, immediately send it to all the social media channels and audiences that you have access to and that are interested in the topic you made your video about. You made this video for them; they're the ones most likely to watch it to the end. Once Google see this, they'll react.

This is important: some people may have friends from church to whom they send their video about their sandwich store... and if the friends don't care – they may still click anyway just to see what crazy Frank is up to – they are not going to watch the video through to the end. You should link to social media that relates to the topic of your video, and in that case you are more likely to get full views.

Twitter links to people interested in the topic that you have written about, which makes great sense as you get immediate clicks and immediate results (nothing is more immediate than Twitter). Embedding pages on Pinterest about your specific topic is also a great way to see some really, really cool results for your YouTube videos from like-minded audience members.

Google+ is good for a number reasons. You don't necessarily get a lot of human traffic looking at the Google+ pages, but you do get Google+ immediately reminding Google of your video's existence - and this is never a bad thing.

If I go to my YouTube homepage, I'll see different friends who have shared content on Google+. These are all people that I'm following on Google+; because they shared things on Google+, those things then showed up on my YouTube page. So yes, people that your audience follows on Google+, whom they follow on YouTube, will still show up on their YouTube homepage. We go into that much deeper in the social media chapter.

Again, immediately send your video to all the social media that's interested in the video you made about topic X.

Number two: if you have a list of people interested in the topic X, you definitely want to email the video link to them. If you don't have a list related to that topic X, and you're marketing on the internet about topic X, build that list. You know more about your audience than any social network ever will (it is, in fact, your social network) and you'll see the best results from the audience you've built.

Now, there has been some training out there in the industry advising you to send members of your list to your blog to watch your videos. That's wrong. Send them straight to YouTube. It's friendly, it's where the nice kitty videos are, and it's where people go to access videos quickly and easily. Definitely send people directly to YouTube the second you go live. Now, once that is done, take the video and embed the video on your blog. This will trigger some people who follow your blog. Again, if you have an email list, send them straight to YouTube. The embedding on the blog is just a secondary alert to Google that you've got content about the topic elsewhere; that is, by embedding the video, you are essentially giving Google a nod that it is about the content at hand.

Finally, encourage everybody to make comments, and do that inside of the video itself. Comments, thumbs up, shares and embeds on other websites send social signals, and the domino effect that comes from that is quite tremendous. Add a social aspect to your videos by encouraging people to comment in your annotations (to reach people watching on their computers) or within the content (for people watching on their phones). This has the double effect of showing the search engines that your content has real engagement, whilst also encouraging others to consume your content in full to see what the commentary was about.

All you have to do is say, "When you're done with this video give us a thumbs up on your phone, computer, or whatever device you are watching us on". Encourage people to make comments and you will do really well. The old "if you don't ask, you won't get" adage is as true here as it has ever been. It will serve you well to respond to any comments that are generated.

That's what you do immediately after publishing your YouTube video in order to ensure you get you the most views and traffic from people who are likely to view it all the way to the end. As a result, Google will see what you're doing, take you seriously and will then start sending more people to you based on the keywords and the topic which your videos concentrate on.

How Do I Get my YouTube Video Ranked on the Front Page of Google?

How do you get your video ranked on the first page of Google results? This one is a lot easier than a lot of pundits would like to make it out be. If you understand the following simple concepts, you can do tremendously well with YouTube and Google results.

Fact number one is that Google is in the business of delivering results. That's their number one job. If they don't deliver good results, people will leave them. Help them do their job and they'll help your videos get seen.

Number two: Google has a massive staff of people whose job is to outfox users who try to trick the results. Obviously, a lot of people who shouldn't be the number one listing for a given search result still want to be the number one listing and are willing to spend time and money to get there. There is a whole industry centered around search engine optimization (SEO), where experts in Google teach people how to manipulate the search engine. Fortunately, Google has hired a substantial staff of very brilliant people – PhD's, gurus and other exceptionally brainy people, some of whom I have met personally – whose job is simply to screen out anybody who is playing tricks.

So tricks can happen, but realize that this is a considerable cat-and-mouse game that I don't recommend playing in any way, shape or form. It's like day trading on the stock market.

Here's the thing: Google likes video more than anything else.

If you do a search on anything and see nine text results and one video option, where are you most likely to click? If you are looking for information, what would you rather do: read or watch? Search engines are a medium of instant gratification and video does a much better job of that. You know this; Google knows this; now it is time to act on what we know.

Now, something that not everybody realizes is that YouTube tracks how long people watch each video. In other words, 10,000 views of a five-minute video where everybody leaves after the first ten seconds of the video, indicates to YouTube that 10,000 people didn't believe this to be a good video about the topic. Fifty people who watched the entire video is considerably better—even five people who watched the entire video is considerably better than 10,000 who stopped after a few seconds.

So Google wants to give its users good results. If they don't they're likely to move to another search engine. Google knows whether or not a result is good based on how long people spend watching the video. If video is a popular choice for a search term and people tend to watch the video all the way through, Google will obviously decide this was an appropriate result for the keywords searched. It's as simple as that.

What can you do with this information?

Make the best video for the Google results you are looking for, to reach an audience who is going to consume the content all the way to the end. If you do that better than anybody else does, you will get ranked on the first page of Google results. That process is actually much easier than cheating the system and playing SEO games - and has a much longer shelf-life. I have videos that are three and four years old seeing more traffic per week now than they did when I first launched and promoted them. You can see the same results.

Google is in the business of getting results and they have a massive staff whose job it is to identify people who are trying to trick them. They track how long people watch each video and they know how good the video is based how long it has been watched. In short, create the best choice for the audience and Google will put you first.

What are the action items?

First, the title for your video should include the keyword that people are looking for. The keyword also needs to be in the first sentence of the description of the video, the tags for the video, and the transcript of the video. Let Google know, as specifically as you possibly can, what your video is about so that they can send some traffic your way to see if you deliver.

Next, you need to make sure that you have a video that people will watch all the way through (to track those statistics, look inside your YouTube analytics). For each video, you can see how long people watch, and you'll see when they drop off as compared to everybody else. If you've got a great video with a keyword-rich title, description, transcript and tags, but you notice that people aren't watching it all the way through to the end, fix your video by adjusting your content. If you do that, you will see some great results and you will see your video on the first page of Google search results. You have about 800 words of content to add to your videos.

New to the book this year is the chapter on "YouTube Automation". It is now possible to do A/B testing on title, keyword and tagging details and I can't recommend the process enough.

Videos Shouldn't be your Only Focus

This doesn't answer the question directly, but it is important to point out that videos aren't the only things that show up in Google results and shouldn't be the entirety of your optimization focus.

YouTube Playlists and Channels both show up in Google and YouTube results. If you are looking for some search engine results, make sure to look there as well.

I personally have a few YouTube Playlists which show up as number one for some very important terms, bringing me great traffic and views. Consider taking on the same strategy yourself (just don't tell my competition!).

A/B Testing

As described in both the "Automated YouTube Marketing" and "Paul's Favorite Tech" chapters, it is possible to do A/B testing on your videos. What does this mean? In short, it simply means that you post two different versions of the same video to see which one gets more of the traffic you are looking for. You can then kill the one which gets the lesser amount and, indeed, have an optimized video page, with a better chance of getting ranked on the first page of Google.

Actually, to be fair, you don't need any automation tools to utilize A/B testing, but they sure make the process easier.

One More Thing … Is Google Everything You Thought It Was?

I could write a book on this topic but it's important to point out that Google, simply, isn't as important as it used to be. At one time, almost all of our traffic came from search engines (and most of that traffic from Google). Now, with Social Media, this is no longer the case.

Yes, do what you can do have traffic that comes from Google -

but don't forget traffic that comes from social media and even email. Take traffic from all possible sources.

What SEO Methods Can I Use to Get my Video Seen?

What are the best SEO methods for a YouTube video? In other words: what can you do, once you've put your video online, to give it the best possibility of getting found?

We know that YouTube looks for the topic of your video to be in each of the following elements of your video: the title (if someone is looking for content about a topic, that topic better be in the title), the description, the keywords and the transcripts. See the chapter on "closed captioning" for transcription options.

If at all possible, it would be of extra value to you to include the topic inside of the channel name too. Let me give you an example. If you have a channel called "Colligan" that features yoga videos, there is no real connection between Colligan and yoga videos (especially if you know me.) But a yoga video and a channel called "Free Yoga Videos" makes a lot of sense. Moreover, getting multiple channels that match up with your content might be something that is worth considering.

So, to recap, include the topic in the title, the description, the keywords, the transcripts and the channel name if at all possible.

We know Google tracks all links online and the keywords associated with them, no matter what kind of content Google is linking to. This is the core of their search strategy and, let's admit, it has worked well for them. As a result, it would be incredibly valuable for you in your YouTube video SEO strategy to include keywords in the link that takes people to your videos. For example, if you have a video called "Free Yoga Workout Video," the link should be called "Free Yoga Workout Video." This is what Google looks for, and it makes sense.

Another effective SEO method for YouTube is embedding videos on sites about that topic. If you embed a YouTube video about yoga (with the topic-rich description, title, transcript, keywords and channel name) on a website about yoga, Google is going to know that your video is a match for that topic - and is therefore much more likely to send people there.

And think about it: if you have a video and several relevant websites containing the link about your topic, doesn't that start to come together for you quite nicely?

Finally, have a video that people watch to the end. This is a tremendously important strategy that can't be overstated. We know that YouTube tracks how far people watch their videos. If you set up the title, the description, the keywords, the transcripts, the channel name, the links and the site that the video is embedded in to reflect a certain topic, but people don't watch the video to the end, it will all have been for nothing. Google will know that you are playing a game - but that your content isn't up to the same standard as the game that you are playing.

What are your action items for optimization?

Number one: figure out the keywords that you want to be found for. Once you decide the keywords that you're looking to be found for inside of YouTube, this realization will let you plan everything out accordingly. A lot of people want to be found for X, but they make a video about Y. They realize they want to be found for X, so they could integrate X into that video, even if that video is a little bit Y.

Again, remember that you want them to watch the video through to the end. Design a video that will be watched all the way through that contains those keywords, and now you have Google validating your work as being both viable and valuable. In fact, editing your video down to size might turn out to be one of your best SEO strategies.

If possible, get the video embedded on sites about that topic. If you're marketing on YouTube about a certain topic I'm going to guess that you probably have sites related to that topic. You might want to work with co-authors and competitors if necessary.

Finally, set up links containing the desired keywords from sites containing the keywords to your YouTube video. Those are the best SEO methods for your YouTube video.

Don't Forget Your Research

Research is key in SEO; for YouTube videos or for anything else. Knowing what your audience is looking for and knowing what works will give you actual goals to optimize for. Sadly, most people publish a video online without the first idea of what they're optimizing for. In the "Automated YouTube Marketing" and "Paul's Favorite Tech" chapters of this book, I examine a number of tools that will let you automate that research process.

How Do I Make my Video Go "Viral"?

I remember that day when he looked me in the eye and said, "Oh, we don't have a marketing budget, we're just going to go viral."

Everybody dreams of making their videos viral, but simply expecting your video to go viral is an absolutely terrible strategy. You've heard the number of hours of content uploaded to YouTube every minute. How many of them are viral? The chances for you to make your video viral is infinitesimally small; it is a terrible strategy. It's like investing in the lottery.

Now if for some reason, your video becomes viral, if a zillion people streamed it, then great; leverage it, take hold of it. But the chances of that are up there with you winning the lottery. It is very hard to plan a viral video; it's just something that you just have to know how to do.

Also, viral videos tend not to be marketing videos. Viral videos usually are not going to be anything that makes anybody money. Indeed, there may even be song rights that come in there as well, further depleting profit. There is really not much bang for the buck in viral video anyway, other than simply the bragging rights.

I once spoke at an event that had a raffle for charity at the evening's close. I offered one of my YouTube training DVD sets and the person who won was surprisingly excited. When I asked why she was so into a YouTube training program, she told me that she had a video that had seen millions of views - but that she had no idea how to make a cent from it - and she was hoping my program would help.

Just because your video goes viral, there is no promise of anything other than bragging rights.

But with that said and done, there are some patterns we can look at here. In truth, what makes a viral video is not complicated. Here are the basic principles:

A viral video is a video where somebody thinks, "I have got to share this". It's the kind of video that creates that visceral response where you just have to share it.

What are the things that people have to share? They have to share really one thing, and that is something entirely unexpected. Nobody shares the expected, and everyone shares the unexpected. If they come to YouTube, they usually see a video they are expecting to see; and the transaction ends there. But if you get them something entirely different than everything else, then you've got a chance that they'll share it.

There are two ways that this happens. One – like a good majority of viral videos – is just humor. People love to be the one that forward along the really funny joke. One of your best chances to add at least some viral elements to your video is just by adding humor - unexpected humor - that people want to share.

The other reason that people pass along a video is something that I've learned from my friend and web videographer Tim Street. Tim says that viral comes from the mixing of two separate strongly contrasting emotions. Think about it; you've seen videos where it's a serene, beautiful moment and then something scary jumps out. Or clips where it's a humorous moment that gets tragic very quickly. Anything where you have contrasting emotions – tragic meets comedic, beautiful meets ugly – these have the best chances of going viral because people don't see it coming. The shock value that comes from the unexpected forces them to pass it along, and it goes viral.

It's also a dirty little secret that a huge amount of the viral video sensations spent millions of dollars getting those initial millions of views. For some, in the end, it was money well spent; but it wasn't the "let's-put-something-up-and-see-it-go-viral" idea that we'd all like to hope/dream it to be.

Please, do the math on viral videos. Just because I watched all of the Old Spice Commercials doesn't mean I changed my deodorant choice and just because I watched a funny Air New Zealand video with the cast of "The Hobbit" doesn't mean I'm going there on vacation any time soon. The real money in online video, and specifically YouTube, is to be made using Google's platform to deliver a message that your specific audience needs. Focus on that, not on "going viral."

What are the action items?

Action number one is very simple: don't worry about going viral, you're probably not going to do that and you're going to fail miserably if that is your plan. It is a really bad strategy despite what I explained here. Instead, worry about matching your video message to your audience; worry about making a video that says what it is that you want to say to the audience that needs to hear it.

Remember, if you have a bunch of folks watching the video for only a few seconds, YouTube simply won't give your video the search-ability or find-ability. Find people who actually are interested in what it is that you have to say and leave the viral to chance.

To confirm and reiterate, don't worry about making things viral - it's really just a bad strategy to sink your teeth into. It's a bit of "hopium", if you will. Work on a video that people will consume so that YouTube knows you're serious about what it is that you're doing.

Sorry to burst your bubble, but that's the sobering truth.

One More Thing About Viral Videos ...

This might surprise you, but, more often than not, the viral videos that you dream of someday making weren't "viral" until , *and yes I have this number right*, tens of millions of views were purchased. It is a common practice in the viral video "space" to purchase enough views to make people treat/view a video as viral. Think about it, if you see a video with a few hundred views, who cares? But, if the video you are looking at has 10 million views before you, how much more likely are you to pass it on?

YouTube is BIG BUSINESS and there is big money that goes into this business. The beauty of YouTube is that with an audience in the billions, you still can be heard above all of the noise and the tens of millions of views purchased to pull eyeballs away from your audience.

Don't try to be the next Psy or PooPourri (if you don't know, don't look them up). Just do what we recommend in this book and match your video with an audience that is looking to see the content it contains.

Is YouTube Really a Social Network? How Should I Respond?

The fact is simple, YouTube is a social network; and you need to plan your approach to YouTube with this in mind.

In early 2014, Google's Eric Schmidt said that "missing the rise of social media was the biggest mistake he had made". Google's complete embracing of social media through the Google+ Platform and their tight integration with several of the networks means that, yes, YouTube is really a social network.

Your response should be the same as YouTube and Google; embrace it fully. What you have at YouTube is so much more than a free video hosting platform. Social media will build your audience in ways a simple subscription paradigm never could.

YouTube is about more than just Google+. YouTube also uniquely ties in closely with other social networks. There are feeds of content and activity streams and all the things that make up a social network are inside. For example, if a user registers their Twitter account with their YouTube account and gives a video a thumbs up, an automatic tweet is generated to Twitter.

Why would Google make YouTube a social network when there are so many? There are a couple of reasons that are really simple if you think about them.

Number one: social equals stick. When you tune in to see the stuff that you've subscribed to or commented on, or to see the community that you're integrating into - that is "stick." You will stay longer and you will come back. Social is stick.

According to YouTube.com, "Millions of subscriptions happen each day. The number of people subscribing daily is up more than 3x since last year, and the number of daily subscriptions is up more than 4x since last year."

Social is stick.

Stick is more money (for YouTube). The longer the people stay, the more ads YouTube can put up. The more interactivity they can get, the bigger the audience they can build. The more they have, the more things they can charge more money for.

So social= stick and stick = more money.

YouTube is smart. Having a video replayed on a page in a network that isn't social is not going to bring them the revenue that they are looking for. It's not going to put them in the strategic position that they are looking for. Remember, YouTube/Google is doing all of this on purpose. Schmidt is not going to repeat his biggest mistake.

So what are the action items? What do you do with this?

Number one: treat YouTube as the social network that it is. Make it as much a part of your marketing efforts as is Twitter, Facebook, Google+ and anything else you might be doing.

Number two: do things that will a bring more viewers as a result of social networking and that will make YouTube more money. What do I mean by this? YouTube makes more money the more subscribers you have, because they come back and they see more videos (YouTube is social). The more money YouTube makes, the more comments you get (the more social interactions that are made), because viewers want to see if somebody commented on their comment (YouTube is social). The more interactivity, the more social networking inside of YouTube, the more money YouTube makes.

In short, the more you do for YouTube, the more YouTube will do for you.

Number three: Get involved inside of Google+. YouTube will leverage the integration to their advantage because… YouTube is social.

I Thought Google+ Was Dead?

In short, Google+ has not gone as well for Google as they hope it would have. There continues to be talk of Google "chopping it up" into different services, or killing it all together.

What does this mean to YouTube and social? Really, nothing …

The Web is still very social and the Internet continues to go in a direction more and more social than anything else. The future of Google+, whatever it may be, has no effect on YouTube's position as a social network of its own, greatly influenced by the interplay of other social networks.

Continue to think social when you think YouTube and continue to integrate it with whatever social network(s) your audience tends to be part of.

What About Social Video Network "X"?

Some of these social networks are including video elements designed, specifically, to compete with YouTube. In some cases you'll want to see your video on these networks as well but there isn't a social network coming that can ever compete with the machine that is YouTube.

How Should I Integrate my YouTube Strategies with Other Social Networks?

YouTube has done a tremendous job integrating with other social media networks, and it's definitely something that you want to leverage. At the time of writing, YouTube integrates directly with Google+, Twitter and Facebook and has great options for linking to social media on your OneChannel page. This list of options will probably change in the future, but the concepts below are true no matter what the list may hold.

What's interesting is that for people who have connected their YouTube accounts with Google+, Twitter and Facebook, many social things will happen automatically. These vary in nature and impact, but they're automatic and result in additional social traffic (and social proof) to your videos and/or channel. One example: if you have linked your YouTube Channel to a Twitter account, and someone who has done the same gives your video a thumbs up, a recommendation will automatically be published on their Twitter feed.

Another example of such automatic integration is the "Social" category under the "What To Watch" menu that will recommend videos shared, liked, mentioned, etc. by friends in connected accounts. A YouTube video liked on Facebook but ignored on YouTube will show up as well.

What does this mean? Why does this matter? You now have a reason to promote your YouTube videos via other social networks. Now, a video liked on Facebook will show up in both the social streams of Facebook AND YouTube. This produces a considerably bigger impact for less effort. Let's face it: it's easier to get a "Like" on Facebook than it is for someone to give you a "Thumbs Up" on YouTube.

It is important to note that (at the time of writing at least) Facebook can only integrate with your personal Facebook account, and not your corporate Facebook page. So this type of integration is something that you'll want to examine further to help you decide whether Facebook integration will be strategic or simply distracting for you.

Google+

You'll note in this book that I'm not a big fan of Google+. I think its impact and usefulness is greatly overstated and I don't see myself changing my mind anytime soon. The integration remains sloppy and hard to work through, despite the millions of dollars they have thrown at it.

I do need to point out that this does not mean you should ignore it in your YouTube Strategies . Google needs Google+ to know what's important and the automatic integration of YouTube with Google+ only means that Google will now send you more of the best possible traffic.

Action Items

What are the action items?

First, simply tie in what social networks make sense. Obviously, since Google+ and Twitter integrate together automatically, those two are an easy decision. As a bonus tip, consider creating a Twitter account for every YouTube channel you have.

However, at this point in time, Facebook only functions with personal account integration. In most cases, when you're using YouTube for marketing purposes, integrating with your personal account won't make sense for your business.

YouTube and Facebook will probably solve this fairly soon, so keep looking into this one.

On your OneChannel, YouTube lets you link to up to four social networks. Pick the four social networks that you use the most and those which your audience tend to use the most, not the ones you think are the most important. For example, if you have no audience on Pinterest, despite what you may hear about how popular it is, don't worry about linking to it.

Remember, YouTube is social. Making sure that everything is integrated for whatever automatic promotion YouTube might offer is an obvious strategic first step. Linking to the social accounts that you frequent the most will give your audience a better understanding of where they can find you - and give these networks the attention they deserve.

How do the Recent YouTube Sponsorship Changes Affect Your Video?

In February of 2015, YouTube amended policies on sponsorships. Instead of letting creators continue to work directly with brands, they now have to run sponsorship deals through Google's sales team. Google then receives an additional revenue source by acting as the conduit between creators and sponsors. This is an important issues that deserves examination - and clarification.

How does this rule affect your specific reality? This one depends on whether or not you run graphical title cards paid for by sponsors at the beginning of your videos. If you do, keep reading; if you don't, consider this short chapter anyway for a larger perspective of working with YouTube and paid product placement.

It is important to note here that the very nature of the Internet, and Google, is CHANGE. I wouldn't have to produce a new version of this book every year if everything stayed the same. Although I can point you in the right direction now and then, I'm not a lawyer, don't play one on TV (or YouTube) and you need to do all of your own research on these kinds of topics. If you register this book, as described in the first chapter, I'll do what I can to keep you up to date with any additional major changes made this year.

The February changes specifically deal with the issue of (PAID) Product Placement inside of a YouTube Video. Specifics can be found here –

https://support.google.com/youtube/answer/154235. It is important to point out that whereas many are claiming and treating this as a new rule, YouTube has stated publically that it is more of an update of existing rules.

It is important to point out that, currently, YouTube allows paid product placement in videos - but simply requires a check to the box that indicates such placement when you are monetizing a video with YouTube. This has been the standard for some time.

The February changes deal mostly with the use of "Title Cards" that run before videos that include logo and branding Some creators have sold this spot for an additional revenue stream directly to sponsors - and this is no longer allowed. A few of the specifics - directly from YouTube:

We allow text-only title cards where there is Paid Product Placement for the purpose of paid product disclosure only. Graphical title cards, including the use of sponsor logos and product branding, are prohibited unless there is a full Google media buyout on the Partner content by the sponsor. You can contact your Partner Manager for more information and assistance.

In short: you can still disclose a relationship with a paid sponsor with text, but not with a product logo or branding, unless the brand pays for that kind of positioning, directly through YouTube. The best estimate for a relationship like this is that YouTube would take approximately 45% of such a deal - effectively half of the take.

Regardless of this change, or any coming changes from YouTube, it is always a best practice to disclose paid placement in any of your videos. In the U.S., the FTC has some very specific rules for online disclosures that I recommend you follow - as this element tends to change on a regular basis, I suggest you search Google *"FTC online disclosures"* for the latest.

Here is my big picture take on this issue: YouTube is and should be allowed to make money on their platform. The infrastructure they provide has made many people a lot of money and they certainly are entitled to their share.

This specific Title Card issue is both a definable element of the sponsorship game, and is also part of the bigger picture of YouTube being able to sell their services without the client looking for a "cheaper" way in. If I, as a brand, have to pay Google to make something specific happen, and there is a known backdoor where I can pay the content creator far less to have them create the same, the relationship quickly becomes antagonistic and takes on a bargain basement mentality. This is good for neither the creator or YouTube.

Will YouTube make further changes? Historically, the answer is yes. Will these affect your chances of making money from YouTube? Again, possibly. However, keep in mind that YouTube needs to keep you as a partner for this delicate dance to work and, as a result, they are forced to keep your best interests in mind as well.

It's not a perfect relationship, like all relationships, but it is based on give and take and continues to mature as time goes on.

Here's a fascinating and very informative video by a YouTuber not thrilled with the rules - but who understands their place –

https://www.youtube.com/watch?v=zoqpBIRtIkw

Should You Consider the YouTube Paid Content Options?

Since the release of the last version of this book, YouTube has opened paid content options to YouTube Channels with 1,000 or more subscribers, which many would consider an easy number to reach. The original requirement was 10,000 users, and it's very possible that YouTube could lower the requirement again this year. Essentially, anyone with a YouTube audience of note has access to the program.

Currently, paid content options are only available in Australia, Brazil, Canada, France, Hong Kong, India, Italy, Japan, Mexico, New Zealand, Philippines, South Korea, Spain, Uganda, United Kingdom, and the United States. More specifics on requirements can be found here - https://support.google.com/youtube/answer/3249165.

What are these premium options, and why do they matter? The most popular option is the ability for channels to open new paid channels that require users to pay to view. Paid channels can be compared to paid television channels in the traditional cable television model, in which where the price per month makes all content available that month. At the time of writing, Google gives 30% of the profits from a paid channel to the creator of the channel. The creator owns all content hosted on a paid channel, and there are no exclusivity requirements that your content be made available only at YouTube.

At the time of writing, there are 291 paid channels at

YouTube, a list of which can be found here:
https://www.youtube.com/channels/paid_channels

In addition to paid channels, creators with more than 1,000 subscribers are also given the option to produce paid videos - videos that customers can either purchase or rent. A purchase or rental involves no physical transaction of goods - it simply makes the video available to the customer through YouTube either for the rental period, or indefinitely if a purchase is made. Although this process may seem foreign to the traditional YouTube user used to free content, it is important to note that the same process and engine is used by YouTube to rent/sell premium movies and television shows. And This process of renting and buying is predicted to become more and more popular as time progresses. Like Paid Channels, Paid Videos give 30% of revenue to the creator.

A 99 cent example of a Paid Video can be found here
https://www.youtube.com/watch?v=4OUwjaYcPTg.

To make a video available for purchase or rental, click to edit the video in YouTube and select "Require rental or purchase to view" in the monetization tab.

When you offer a video for rental or purchase, YouTube lets you pick the pricing and age rating for each video. At the time of writing, YouTube requires an entry for every rental and purchase price in every country. This process can be a bit tedious in nature (especially if you want to sell your video in multiple countries - even English speaking ones). However, if you don't set your video rating, YouTube will assume that your video is for adults only, which can result in some embarrassing assumptions or awkward questions at tech support.

Payment at YouTube for rental or purchase requires a Google Wallet account. While this is the same account Android

Phone users need to emulate the features of Apple Pay, funded Google Wallet accounts are, at this point, a rarity.

The real question you should be asking is this: Is the Premium model for content something that you should consider? The impact of reach of YouTube is without question, however the question of whether or not YouTube's audience will be willing to pay for content when so much other content is available for free still needs to be examined. When you add the extra steps required for a Google Pay account for access, it is difficult to believe that enough of an audience is there to make this a financially viable model at this point in time.

Online media is always a question of market to media. The market for YouTube at this point continues to be people looking for free content, expecting to find an audience willing to pay for your content. I cannot recommend this business model at present, but this could change in the future. However, at this point I don't recommend this strategy.

The one strategy for paid YouTube content or a paid channel worth considering is the social proof that this type of relationship with YouTube can carry in certain audiences. I've used the example above of my pay-per-view video as an example of how my channel carries a certain gravitas within YouTube that not everyone has. Being able to "sell" at YouTube puts me in a league different from a lot of my competitors. You would be surprised how many YouTube gurus and authors don't have the numbers for some of the advanced features mentioned here. If such positioning is valuable to you or your company, now or in the future, you might want to make a paid video for channel available. If you're worried about how a paid channel with an audience of two would look, that that It is possible to "turn off" your audience count to the general public.

At this point, a positioning play for YouTube paid content is the only model I can recommend. Register this book, as described in the first chapter, and I promise to update you this year if anything changes worth noting.

Automated YouTube Marketing

Phil Starkovich is the only name I trust in tools specifically designed for Automated YouTube Marketing. When you read this chapter, you'll understand why.

Automated YouTube Marketing

Automated YouTube marketing is a safe, simple and effective way to get more views, subscribers and engagement on your YouTube channel and videos.

Most systems work by automating actions that would have otherwise been done manually. For example, let's say you sell a product for surfers. You might spend your day doing searches on YouTube and contacting people who have commented on surf-related videos. When done manually, that could easily fill up several hours of your day. But, when done through an automated system, the same task can be done in minutes. That is, it might take just minutes to set up some parameters, push 'Start' and then the system runs 24 hours per day for you, doing the searches and contacting people. Automated marketing systems work for you while you work on more important things.

There are two basic types of automation. Automation using the YouTube API and automation using browser emulation.

YouTube API Automation

Just like Facebook and Twitter, YouTube wants people to build applications that enhance their user's experiences. In order to allow people to build applications that hook into their website, YouTube offers a public API. API stands for Application Programming Interface and is a simple, consistent way that developers can work with YouTube in any programming language. For full details on the YouTube API and what they offer, visit: https://developers.google.com/youtube/ .

The main benefit of products built using the YouTube API is stability. When using the API, changes to the YouTube public website will not affect any products that connect to YouTube through their API. This means that with each new feature rolled out or homepage change, you have nothing to worry about. The product will continue to work as expected.

The main drawback of YouTube marketing through their API is that you're limited by what the API offers. For example, the API offers a way for you to share a video with other users on YouTube but does not offer a way for you to send a message to other users. It seems a bit arbitrary as to what YouTube decided to include and leave out, but at least the majority of features made it in.

TubeAssist

http://www.PaulColligan.com/TubeAssist

TubeAssist is by far the best product on the market for automating YouTube marketing through the YouTube API. It can be used on any device that has a web browser: Windows, Mac, phones, tablets or computers.

It's extremely easy to get started with TubeAssist. After creating an account, all you need to do is enter a search phrase and select a campaign type. The available campaign types are: add contacts, share videos and subscribe to channels. TubeAssist will then automatically perform a search on YouTube for the phrase that you enter and creates a list of users who have commented on videos in the search results. Depending on what campaign type you selected, it then starts adding each person as a contact, sharing a video with them or subscribing to their channel. TubeAssist continues this process 24 hours per day, sending at a safe rate.

Your video and/or channel will start showing up in the inboxes of thousands of targeted YouTubers. As they click to view your channel and videos you'll not only see your views increase, you'll also find more engagement and subscribers than ever before. The best part is that it really only takes minutes to set up and can then run for months on its own.

For more details, visit TubeAssist's website:

http://www.PaulColligan.com/TubeAssist

Browser Emulation

Browser emulation is the alternative to YouTube API automation and is a fairly simple concept. Anything that you can do manually on YouTube.com's website can be emulated through programming code. For example, if you share a video through YouTube's website, you first click the 'Share' link, then type in the recipient's username, then click the 'Send' button. Each of those three steps can be re-created and executed programmatically. As far as YouTube knows, it looks to them like a real person was sitting down at a computer and clicked the share button, entered a username then clicked the send button.

There are many benefits to choosing browser emulation over API programming; mainly, that you can basically automate anything that you do on YouTube.com's website. You're not limited to the feature set that they make available through the API. In fact, in some cases you can do even more that what is offered on YouTube's website by entering values through code in areas where there is no user input on the screen for regular users using a browser.

One downside of browser emulation is that it is heavily dependent on screen scraping. Screen scraping means that the program loads a webpage, reads through the source code of the page and then takes an action based on what it finds. If YouTube changes the way a screen looks or acts it could potentially break the browser emulation software and require a fix. Make sure that if you go with a browser emulation product, you stick with a company that stays on top of YouTube changes.

The Automated Marketing Process

Whether you use API or browser emulation, there are two basic steps to automation. The first step is to choose which users on YouTube to contact ("gathering") and the second step is to actually contact them ("sending").

Gathering

The first step of an automated system is to collect a group of YouTube users who will be contacted later. This is called "gathering". When gathering, it's imperative that you target your ideal demographic. Because YouTube limits the number of actions you take per day, each one counts and you don't want to waste it on someone outside your demographic. The best group of users to gather are people who have commented on videos similar to yours. If someone has commented on a video similar to yours, it means that not only would they be interested in your content but they are also active in the YouTube community (because they made a comment).

Sending

There are several ways to contact and generate interest from the people who you have gathered. Each type will have a different impact and each one has its own set of restrictions imposed by YouTube.

Sharing Videos

When you share a video, the video shows up in the user's YouTube inbox. Depending on their privacy settings, it will also likely show up in their personal email inbox. This puts your video right in front of their face. Sharing videos is a great choice when you're promoting a single video and want to get more views for that video. When using the browser emulation method, you are limited to approximately 400 videos shared per day; whereas using the API, you are limited to approximately 250 per day.

Adding Contacts

Adding someone as a contact is great way to reach out in an unobtrusive fashion. When users see that you have added them as a contact, they are likely to take a look at your channel which will hopefully lead to gaining general views with an even distribution across your videos. YouTube does not limit the number of people you can add per day as a contact. However, your contacts list only shows your first 5,000 contacts.

Sending Messages

When you send a message to another user on YouTube, it shows up directly in their inbox. It can include URLs (although not hyperlinked) and is a great personal way to connect with other YouTubers. Sending messages is only available in browser emulation software, not YouTube API applications. YouTube is very restrictive as this feature could lead to spam; as a result, you can only send about 200 messages out per day.

Subscribing to Channels

When you subscribe to other channels on YouTube, there is a good chance that many of those people will subscribe back. It's a great way to gain new subscribers as well as make some random people happy. It's a win-win. The speed at which you can subscribe to other channels is not limited; however, you are limited to a total of 2,000 subscriptions unless you yourself have a big following i.e. more than 2,000 people subscribed to your channel.

Safety

YouTube makes it clear in their Terms Of Service that automation is allowed; however, you must not access their website faster than a human could using a conventional web browser.

http://www.youtube.com/static?template=terms

Article 4 Section H:

You agree not to use or launch any automated system, including without limitation, "robots," "spiders," or "offline readers," that accesses the Service in a manner that sends more request messages to the YouTube servers in a given period of time than a human can reasonably produce in the same period by using a conventional on-line web browser.

Products that you can trust (like Tube Toolbox and TubeAssist) strictly follow these rules without exception. In fact, Tube Toolbox has a video series where they have recorded themselves doing each action manually with a timer and then based their application against those proven results.

If your channel and videos showcase prohibited, stolen or copyrighted content, then you are subject to being suspended no matter what type of automation you are using. In addition, YouTube seems to not bother people with legitimate channels and real content. The only cases that people have run into rare issues with automation is those who use channels that contain no videos, no subscribers and no views and simply use them to spam. If your channel doesn't have any real content and you are just using it to spam, then use automation at your own risk.

Keep in mind that browser emulation and API programming are completely different than purchasing views. If you go to a website that sells views, you are greatly at risk of getting your channel suspended. Many channels that sell views will give you false views that are not generated by real people but instead browser tricks and drone computers churning out inflated numbers. YouTube has a strict policy against this type of action and you can easily get videos taken down or your channel suspended if you purchase views.

Summary

You spend enormous amounts of time creating, editing and uploading videos to YouTube. With tools like Tube Toolbox and TubeAssist, you can now put your YouTube marketing on autopilot and get your videos seen with very little effort. You'll be able to put your time and energy into creating quality content, not promoting it.

When choosing which type of automation and product to go with, make sure to read reviews, contact their support teams and get a sense for what you can trust. With the right product, you'll be able to gain views and new subscribers while you sleep.

New Tools For 2015

Since this article was written, Phil and his team have introduced two other tools that follow the rules and practices laid out in this chapter.

On the Cloud side - and using APIs correctly is **Video LC** (http://www.PaulColligan.com/VideoLC).

And perhaps even more important - **Tube Buddy** - a browser plugin (extension) for Chrome that makes it possible to automate the things that should be automated, while keeping the process in line with YouTube terms and conditions. More information about Tube Buddy can be found at http://PaulColligan.Com/TubeBuddy.

What are the Best Third Party Tools and Services for YouTube?

Note: I have a full chapter on "YouTube Automation" that goes into the topics in here in much greater detail. I also have a "Paul's Favorite Tech" chapter that puts everything together in one place (with all the links that matter). If you are going to enter the world of automation, and I highly recommend that you think about doing so, you'll want to check out that chapter as well.

*New For 2015: Take a look at **TubeBuddy*** (http://www.PaulColligan.com/TubeBuddy). This "little" tool is a simple plugin for Chrome that enables some of the most sophisticated YouTube Marketing I've ever seen. It is, in short, the perfect integration of the automation YouTube allows with the human elements required. The company that produces TubeBuddy is one that I highly recommend and this tool is one of the most powerful third party tools I've ever seen. Because they are browser based, they follow all of the YouTube rules and requirements I explain in this chapter.

You may have searched the internet, seen videos or read articles claiming that there are third-party tools and services that you can use with YouTube. To be honest, there was a time when many of these tools worked surprisingly well. There are still a few out there (and new ones that pop up now and then) that produce some interesting results; but it is, at best, a murky river to play in.

Remember, YouTube can shut down your account if they feel you aren't playing by the rules.

Should you consider third party tools? Avoid them? What should you do? What should your strategy be?

Consider this: at the time of publication of this book, YouTube terms and conditions say specifically that you cannot use any software that accesses their servers faster than a human can in the same amount of time. They are not against robots, mechanics or automation, but they are against automation mechanics that act faster than a human. I link to the YouTube Terms in the "Additional Web Resources" so you can see this for yourself. *This area of the terms hasn't changed in years.*

Those are YouTube's rules – and it's something that you can debate until the end of time if you wish – but you have agreed to play by them. Break them, and YouTube can, and will, shut you down. YouTube doesn't want your tools to go faster than a human can, so quite simply, don't use anything that goes faster than a human can.

Don't use tools that don't act like a human does. at least until YouTube changes their terms. Register your book, as described at the beginning of this book, and we'll make sure to update you if and when they do.

YouTube has an API for users that freely admit they are a machine. YouTube is fine with machines and software, but you definitely need to use their API, because you don't want to pretend to be anything other than what you really are. This one isn't specifically in the terms, but in my experience, don't use a tool that doesn't use the YouTube API.

What is an API? API stands for Application Program Interface and it's a way for one computer to talk to another very effectively. That's it. You don't need to know how it works, you just need to know that any tool you use ,for publishing or anything else, uses the YouTube API.

Basically, you don't want YouTube to ever start to think, "Is this viewer not real in some way? Is there something else we need to worry about?" You don't want any question marks associated with your account; be transparent with them, as you would any partner.

Based on my experience – I'm not a lawyer, and I don't play one on TV either – anybody who follows the rules of YouTube's Terms of Service and uses the API for third-party software doesn't experience any problems. Again, that's my experience.

However, you still need to think smart. If you use a tool with the API to upload a bunch of videos that are viewed for five seconds, that will only result in a low quality score and could bring you more damage than good. You might get 1,000 views, but if your video never comes up in the search results for those 1,000 views, does it really matter?

More important than any tool, you need to match the right audiences to your videos, the ones that will actually be interested in viewing your content. Don't just try to bump up your numbers to make mom feel proud of that click count. Using third-party tools and services is one method to boost your click count, but use it wisely and follow YouTube's rules to avoid being blocked. .

In terms of the key question - which are the best ones to use - I list them all in the "Paul's Favorite Tech" chapter.

What Should I Do About the New YouTube Live Options?

Just a few years back, going "live" on the internet with video was a very expensive proposition. Yes, it was amazing that you could reach the whole world without the assistance (or geographical requirements) of an expensive transmitter, but it certainly wasn't within reach of the average Joe or Jane. I've been part of several live broadcasts that have generated considerable profit and I wouldn't have changed a thing, but I have also sent checks to some technology partners in the five-figure-region for the "honor" of just a few hours live.

A few years before that, it was just a dream.

Those days are gone. Now, anyone with a Webcam and a connection to the Internet can broadcast live to the world thanks to the advent of YouTube.

This reality should be your top YouTube strategy! It's both a way to grab attention *now* and create great content for *later*. Some of my most popular and profitable YouTube videos are the archives of a video that was originally created live.

The Urgency of Live

Let's face it, you probably have a stack of books you intend on reading, a number of Podcast episodes you hope to consume soon, and hundreds of emails in a folder that you are going to read later. It's a busy world and the tyranny of urgency all too often forces us to put anything that we can postpone on hold.

The same is true for YouTube videos. On a daily basis I see a video that I plan to come back to but never get around to doing it. You know the rest of the story.

But live changes everything. If my option for consumption is Tuesday night at 8pm or nothing at all, the chances I'll be there at 8pm are considerably higher. Use this to your advantage. Throw in the fact that your audience can consume on pretty much any connected device, and ... wow.

A Brief History of YouTube Live

When YouTube first launched "YouTube Live" it was something that only the TOP YouTube partners could get into. It was one of those "it's-who-you-know" situations. I had associates with millions and millions of views under their belt who were waiting just to hear back from YouTube about their status; so of course, I never thought I'd get access to the platform so quickly.

When Google introduced Google+, they knew they needed a "killer app" to bring people into the system. This was their Google Hangout brainchild which utilized a great amount of YouTube technology, but wasn't at all integrated with the platform. Google Hangouts, for the completely uninitiated, is essentially a video "chat room", where up to ten people can connect together with shared webcams. Not only was the technology very impressive, but it required no additional software other than a small browser plug-in.

Then, one day, Google announced *Google Hangouts On Air* - which meant that people could "broadcast" their hangouts using, surprisingly enough, the YouTube engine. It was, essentially, a back door to broadcasting live on YouTube; and a LOT of marketers quickly embraced this.

A few months after this "back door" option became obvious, YouTube reopened the YouTube Live option to anyone who had 1,000 subscribers or more. Recently they changed it to

100 subscribers or more. Hangouts have always had no subscriber restrictions.

Now, All you need is an account with Google to proceed.

Live With Google Hangouts On Air

Initially, Google Hangouts On Air acted a lot like YouTube Live - but it was more restricted in impact and more hidden from general view. You couldn't "schedule" an event, you could only broadcast in standard definition and you could tie your broadcasts into your YouTube Channel page. Once you set up a Google Hangout On Air, you were able to get a direct link that you could broadcast however you wanted, and an embed code that let you put your video on any web page to which you had access.

The other limit to Hangouts On Air was that they were only available as a public event, so if you only wanted a select group to be able to access your content, there was nothing you could do to stop someone who was looking for your event to find it - let alone prevent that unauthorized individual from watching.

Live With YouTube Live

Describing the difference between YouTube Live and Google Hangouts On Air is difficult because not only are the differences very nuanced, they also are changing on a regular basis. In 2013, I recorded four different training videos, intended for publishing to some of my students and clients, that I had to delete before I could ever publish because of the rapid changes being made at YouTube. I promise you, whatever I write here will most certainly change in some way before you read it - so make sure you register this book as described in the "About this Book" section so I can make sure to update you throughout the year.

With that said and done, the basic difference between

Hangouts On Air and YouTube Live is simple: Hangouts On Air looks, feels, and acts like a chat room, while YouTube Live is more like a traditional broadcasting platform. Whereas all you needed for Hangouts was a web browser, you needed additional software for YouTube Live; and where a Hangout was something you just clicked and started, YouTube Live required scheduling the event ahead of time.

Now ...

At the time of writing, both Hangouts and YouTube Live Events can be started from the same page at YouTube (http://www.YouTube.com/my_live_events). Both have options defining who can access the content, and both let you schedule either kind of broadcast from the same interface. As we've seen historically, Hangouts can still be done from the web browser and Live Events still require additional third-party software.

Again, I heavily stress the constant fluctuation of this element of YouTube and again recommend your registration of this book so I can keep you up to date all year.

What Are My Mobile Options?

At the time of writing, there are no mobile options of initiating or running a Google Hangout On Air or YouTube Live Event from a mobile device. There are some options for participating in a Hangout through the Hangouts App for both Android and iOS, but they are limited in functionality and stability.

Surprisingly enough, if mobile options for live streaming are a necessity to you, there are options from both Ustream.tv and Livestream.com that will let you broadcast from a mobile device.

On the flip side, all current YouTube Live and Hangouts On Air video is optimized for viewing on all mobile devices.

YouTube does this very, very well.

What's Best?

So, what's best? Hangouts On Air or YouTube Live?

If 1080p Video is required, you only have one choice - YouTube Live. If you want the best HD video possible, it is currently not offered on Hangouts.

Hangouts currently embed a Google "bug" (an overlay in the broadcast video) during your Hangouts On Air. If this is unacceptable, YouTube Live is your only option.

If you don't have the software or equipment to do a live broadcast, you'll want to stick with Hangouts On Air.

If you want to interact with multiple users in multiple locations during your broadcast and don't have the considerable budget that traditional methods would require, you'll need to stick with Hangouts On Air.

Once these vital considerations are made, the decision becomes a matter of choice. Generally, if you are more the do-it-yourselfer, the all-in-one style of Hangouts On Air makes it much easier to run an event from your laptop. If you are doing a more professional broadcast with a more traditional talent/producer distribution of tasks, YouTube Live might be the best option for you.

Please Don't Miss This - Hangout Events Versus YouTube Live

YouTube has spent a considerable amount of time and effort expanding the Google+ platform. Google+ now has a number of features and options that expand the Google Hangout, and they continue to offer reasons and incentives to use Google+ as a destination. These are, at best, mere distractions; and sadly, all too often, they are a really bad idea.

Yes, I am not a big fan of the Google Hangouts Platform, but this is not a book about Google Hangouts. If this is the platform you are looking to focus on, take a look at the "Additional Resources" chapter at the end of this book. I've got some great options for you.

What I want to talk about here are the incentives – or the distractions – that Google Hangout Events offer to someone looking to leverage live video on YouTube.

The biggest issue at play is that Google Hangout Events require that your audience be on the Google+ platform, utilizing the tech it brings to the table. Now, while the tech is very impressive, it's not nearly as impressive as the simplicity offered by YouTube Live. Google Hangout Events require your audience to be logged into Google+ with a Google+ account, while YouTube Live merely requires a connected device with YouTube capabilities. Why offer your content only to people in front of their computers who are familiar with Google+ (which is a number far less impressive than Google or the Google+ evangelists will lead you to believe), when you can offer your content to a Blackberry user on the bus, a housewife at home with a connected television set, a student with a tablet (whichever platform; it doesn't matter), and a knowledgeable worker who happens to be in front of his/her computer? Live video is about reach.

As this is a book about strategies, I must stress the need to distinguish the opportunity of live video (distributed by YouTube for free) from the layers of complexity others like to place around it.

Which Is Better?

New For 2015 - I suspected this for a long time, but I never had confirmation - until now. I believe (and have heard) that although they both use YouTube as transport, the engine behind YouTube Live and Google Hangouts On Air are, in fact, different engines all together. I've also been lead to believe (by more than one source) that the YouTube Live engine is, simply, more robust and capable than the Hangouts engine. This matches my experiences - and I've done dozens of live events to tens of thousands of viewers.

What do you do with this news? Why does it matter? Because there is no barrier of entry to using YouTube Live, consider making it your choice.

Best Practices for Live Video

Imagine telling your audience "You can catch me live on YouTube this Thursday at 8 pm." With all the questions of Hangouts versus Live and which option is best, nothing beats the simple statement above. Yes, you've been able to go live on other platforms for some time, but none of them came even close to a percentage of the reach offered by YouTube - let alone the cache that comes with such a statement.

And remember, this isn't just YouTube.com on the den computer; this is phones, gaming platforms, tablets, connected televisions, etc.

Who would you rather reach: people in front of a computer, or people in front of any screen connected to the internet?

This may seem a bit odd when talking about video, but audio is more important than anything else. Less than perfect video with decent audio is watchable. Even the best video won't be watched if the audio is bad. A microphone that makes you sound good is your first investment. If you want suggestions, check out the "Paul's Favorite Tech" chapter at the end of this book.

Before we talk cameras, the issue of lighting comes next. A well-lit camera shot will have a better impact on your audience than a fancy-pants camera will. What's the best way to set up lighting? Do a search (on YouTube) for "3-point lighting".

Finally, and obviously, get the best camera you can afford. Many laptops now come with HD cameras that are surprisingly good. I currently broadcast on a $250 consumer camcorder with a $150 adapter. I don't want to put the specifics here because I'm sure my choice will change by the time you read this - so make sure you register this book.

When broadcasting live, there often is an urge to do everything yourself. This is because, quite simply, you can do so with the software available to you for free. A single person running Hangouts On Air has the ability to choose camera shots, run the chat room, add special effects, bring in new guests, add/change lower third graphics, and more. Whereas the list of capabilities is impressive, there is no more boring video than watching someone click buttons on their computer and complain when things go wrong.

Consider a 'producer' for your live events. Let someone else handle the technical issues while you handle the content. If you can't, consider bringing only as much tech as you can handle to your events and letting the fancy aspect take second base to the content.

I guarantee your first live event will be your worst live event. I guarantee your second worst will be your second. Can you see where I'm going here? The best thing about Hangouts On Air is that you can start practicing now, and, if needed, you can always delete your results.

Number one: utilize this tool in all of your marketing efforts and in everything you do. The ability to say, "Watch me live on YouTube" carries a tremendous amount of cache. Just imagine having the ability to tell your list that you'll be live on YouTube every Friday to answer questions, or on any one day at a specific time. Broadcasting live should definitely be part of your plan.

The second point is that if you do hold a live event and you feel that it didn't go well, know that you can delete any video from your video archive. It's not difficult to do, and it's perfectly natural.

Your third action item is to understand that this is the future of internet video. Internet video is going live—and the ability to interact, to be social, to ask questions, and to know that you are in the same time and place as the person consuming the video, is what lies ahead. You absolutely need to take part in this, and make it part of your business and marketing. That's how you make best use of the new YouTube live options.

Options

Here is a graphic that should help you understand the technical differences and similarities in the two services. Obviously, this can change at any point:

When Should I Use YouTube and the YouTube Player? When Should I Not?

This is a great question asked by many. A lot of people think, "If you put up a video on YouTube, people can click over to YouTube, or can find related videos about my competitors. With the YouTube player, people can do all sorts of things that they shouldn't do (or, more accurately, that I don't want them to). Yes, the YouTube player is easy - but I don't want to use it for those reasons."

Having reasons for your actions is a good thing, but let's make sure we work this one all the way through. Let's review the facts.

YouTube is extremely friendly, safe, familiar and works on every machine, phone and tablet. The fancy video player that you put on your website might not work on the very device that people are looking at. I've yet to see any other video player on the market that works with absolutely everything. Nothing is more frustrating than visiting a website that says "Click here to play" and then finding it does not work.

Since YouTube is going to work on every machine, phone and tablet, you can put that on your website and rest assured that the content has the best possible chance of being consumed. If this isn't your goal, ask yourself why not? Use YouTube's player and you are not going to be producing frustration in your customer and audience base as they try to make someone else's software work. Nobody ever looks at a video player and thinks that their codec might not be supported;

they simply think your video is broken.

You should understand that more often than not, the positives of having the YouTube player are going to outweigh the negatives. If you use a fancy video player that people don't know how to use, they might struggle just to find the play button (you'd be surprised). Appreciate that your audience has done YouTube before, so your audience knows YouTube. Integrating the YouTube player into your website is going to make the experience easy and familiar; it's going to be exactly what people are familiar with. People love familiarity.

YouTube gives the strongest rankings to the videos that people actually watch all the way through; that's the number one ranking variable today. The best way to do that is to offer them a video where they can see exactly how long the video is going to be before beginning. People love to know what to expect. If people know exactly the experience they are going to get, then you have a better chance of them watching your content through to the end – or, conversely, not watching at all (which has no negative effect on your rankings).

People from your site are the ones most likely to watch your videos all the way to the end, because people from your site are the ones who like you the most. Putting a YouTube player on your site or blog brings the familiarity of YouTube to the relationship offered by your site for a powerful combination you just can't get from another fancy player.

However, you should not use the YouTube player when you're doing something extremely commercial that will get you banned from YouTube. Look up the community standards at YouTube, which tell you quite clearly what you can and cannot do. If you have a video that's going to break the rules, then definitely don't do it. It's counterproductive to get yourself banned. In light of all the work you did to get your video on YouTube, doing something silly like this just doesn't make sense. So, in this case, use the third party video player; but honestly, you still might want to use one that looks like YouTube.

Finally there is a decision to make: Does the possibility of viewers leaving your site by clicking on the link inside the YouTube player outweigh the benefits of using the YouTube player? If the chance of them leaving is that big and that dangerous (I really have found very few times that it actually is), then put up your own player. But when it comes down to it, at least nine times out of ten, using the YouTube video player on your site is going to make a lot more sense. This is something you can easily test with some decent web analytics software.

Once again, the action items are simple:

Use the YouTube video player whenever you possibly can. And also, realize you can check or uncheck the option to "Show suggested videos" so that at least you will not be automatically promoting somebody else at the end. Do use the YouTube player whenever you can because the positives usually outweigh the negatives.

I need to close this with a warning to remind you of the massive market of people finding solutions to problems that don't really exist. If you're looking at using a third-party player (and there are times when you should), ask yourself if their goal is to help you in your efforts, or sell you a piece of software. The answer to that question alone solves this issue for many.

Is It Better to Have One YouTube Channel for Everything I Do?

This is a question that I get asked all the time, and it's a great strategy question that absolutely makes sense - especially when starting to develop your YouTube Strategies . Starting smart is always better than fixing things later. Is it better to have one YouTube channel for everything or a separate YouTube channel for every niche you happen to find yourself involved with?

Let's walk through what we know here:

YouTube accounts are free. It's not that difficult to sign up for a different account or channel, because they are free and because the option is always there. We certainly don't see that changing.

YouTube used to put a lot of emphasis on how much action and how many videos your channel had.

We now know that YouTube puts more weight on how long the videos are viewed than anything else. Therefore, the benefit of having a channel with a lot of views isn't as strong as it used to be. If you're looking to the future and tracking where things are going, you are going to find that this type of focus is becoming more and more pronounced - i.e., channels aren't as important as they used to be.

There were some significant benefits of subscriber and view numbers for your channel in the old YouTube Partner Program, which seems to have all but disappeared. In the latest implementation of the program, if you place an ad on any of your YouTube videos, you are basically a partner. At the time of publication, the only benefit for subscriber and channel view numbers comes from consideration for larger content networks, audience requirements for live streaming or subscriber level expectations for paid channels.

All in all, these realities point to the limited negatives of having different channels for different niches, unless you are looking for one of the goals mentioned in the last paragraph.

Moreover, there are actually a few benefits of having multiple channels.

Remember that you can cross-promote channels. If you have five channels, each of the five channels can promote back to one channel, and you can create a network. There are certainly some internal ranking features that exist there.

Also, keep in mind that it is considerably easier to promote people to a certain channel about a certain topic. For example, I send people to my YouTube Channel "Colligan", which is something that I created and named a long time ago that has too many views to let go of. But think about it; what is "Colligan" about? Were I to have called the channel something along the lines of "YouTube Training" or "Internet Marketing Videos," my potential audience would know exactly what to expect.

Now, I also have a YouTube channel called "Paul's iPad." That one is easy: it's about iPads. Making a channel name specific to its material will let people know exactly what's there, and won't waste people's time. If you're matching your videos to an audience, they will watch them to the end; it just makes sense.

However, bear in mind that people can get very easily distracted when they are managing a myriad of channels. I've seen people who have spent 80% of their week managing all their YouTube channels, and only 20% creating content. For goodness' sake, spend your time on content and don't worry too much about these things.

Is it better to have one channel for everything or one per niche? I would say one per niche, unless that's going to be a distraction for you... and that's something only you can answer.

When Should I Let YouTube Place Ads on my Videos?

"YouTube asks about placing ads on my videos. YouTube talks about partnering with me. When should I let YouTube place ads on my videos? Is the money any good?"

Well, the first thing I want to point out – and this is just a simple fact – is that the money from advertising YouTube videos is negligible. There is no other way to put it. It's just not viable for most. Yes, there are times when one might want to become a "YouTuber" and there is certainly some great money to be made in it, but the majority of those of you reading this book haven't gotten to the point that your checks from YouTube will pay your mortgage.

Without breaking any rules here, I can tell you that one of my channels has seen more than 14,000 views in the last month. A percentage of them have ads, and my revenue from those ads looks to be a bit more than $71. Yes, I'll cash that check, but it's a small, small part of why I'm on YouTube.

In short, my monetization strategies for YouTube are bigger than getting a few dollars every time a thousand people watch one of my videos. There is certainly money in the numbers, but that is not where I wish to make my money.

Letting YouTube place ads on your videos just for the cash doesn't make sense unless you go viral or you're just the type of person who has millions of people viewing your videos. If you can pull that off, great. But in reality, ads are just a lot more work and a lot more effort than many people make it out to be.

There is a strategy to letting YouTube put ads on your videos that you really want to think about. For instance, when Google has no sponsored video for your term, they might actually put up your video as a sponsored video if it has an ad on it. Why? Because that ad makes them money. I've seen this happen for my own videos time and time again.

Think about it, let's imagine your term is "Glass Houses", and they don't have any sponsored videos for glass houses. Consequently, you have a video about glass houses that has an ad on it. Guess what? YouTube makes money if your video shows up in sponsored results. I have seen that happen, and I have seen thousands of views every month come simply by placing ads on specific videos.

Honestly, I have yet to see an ad that distracts my audience. Though I've never seen a competitor's ad in any of my videos, but that is possible, and you might want to monitor the ads for quality assurance. I have seen thousands of views brought in by YouTube as a result of this strategy, so keep it in mind.

Again, you should realize that YouTube makes money from the ads. As a result, YouTube looks at all the partners and says, "Which of the partners have I made money from? Which of the channels have I made money from?" Those are the ones that they are going to promote the most. So if you include ads on a couple of videos, you are going to do better on your YouTube channel than people who don't.

What are your action items related to letting YouTube place ads on your videos?

Regardless of what you do, throw ads on one or two videos. The protection that comes from doing so is never a bad thing. YouTube will see you as a player, as a member of the team, and your video will be viewed every once in awhile. In fact,

I've known people who have put up videos for the specific purpose of housing ads, just to distract YouTube from the content that they don't put ads on.

In addition to this, you are required to monetize at least one video to get some of the benefits of YouTube sponsorship.

Finally, check your video for the terms on which it will be centered, and see if there are any other sponsored ads that come up. If there are, and they're exactly on your topic, you might want to reconsider your plans.

If there aren't any sponsored videos on your keywords or topic, it means that if you put an ad on your video, there is a chance that it could become a sponsored video. Just by virtue of this, you will get more clicks from people specifically looking for content about your topic. It's a great way to get you to the top of the list without special optimization efforts, and it kills two birds with one stone.

Besides, a check or two, even if it only buys you pizza, is never a bad thing.

Let YouTube place ads on your videos, but only if it's advantageous to you. Think of the big picture, think long-term, and you will do quite well.

How to Monetize Online Videos With Webcasts – Live Interactive Online Videos You Can Produce for Free - By Mike Koenigs

Mike Koenigs is a previous collaborator/co-author, former employer, and, most importantly dear friend. I'll never forget the day I told him "Hey, I really think we should start doing all of our Webcasts on YouTube LIve ..." The following is a chapter from his coming book "Webcast Profit Toolkit: How to Build, Engage and Monetize Your Audience with Live Interactive Online Video Shows."

I couldn't write a book of YouTube Strategies without mentioning Webcasts and I couldn't think of a better primer on the topic than this. Do remember, everything Mike discusses in this chapter can be done with YouTube Live, for free ...

What if I told you it's possible to earn a million dollars in less than a day with a "webcast" – an interactive online video program you can produce for free from the comfort of your living room or office?

With nothing more than a mobile phone or tablet, laptop computer and a webcam, you can broadcast to a limitless audience in minutes. If you have a bigger budget, you can set up a more advanced system that rivals the quality of a network television station.

The best way to describe a webcast is it's a direct to camera infomercial that can be any length, made with any equipment and educate, demonstrate, entertain one or more people and incorporate some form of interactive chat to directly communicate with the viewer.

Webcasts – also known as livecasts or livestream events can be produced free of charge and educate, entertain, build loyalty, trust, connection and can be used to sell virtually any product or service to practically anyone in any industry.

At some point during the webcast "show", you tell your viewers to click a button, go to a web page, text or call a phone number to take action and buy yours or someone else's product.

If this sounds intriguing to you, then keep reading because I'll share with you how this is possible even if you don't know much about video, you're not a techie or don't think you look or sound great on camera.

If you don't believe this is possible or even true, it's good to be skeptical. If you invest a few minutes and continue reading, perhaps you'll experience an intuitive "ah-ha" moment that will help you cross over and become a believer.

The Opportunity of a Lifetime

Let me put the power of webcasts in perspective for you.

Right now over half of the population of the planet has Internet access and can watch videos or podcasts from their smartphones, tablets, computers or smart televisions.

The question to ask yourself is what are you doing right now to build your brand, engage with this nearly limitless audience and encourage them to connect with your or buy your products and services?

More importantly, are you going to miss out on what is the best time in human history to take advantage of an opportunity to connect and grow your visibility and reach while building your reputation and wealth almost for free?

After coaching and selling online marketing services and products to over 40,000 small business owners, authors, experts, speakers, consultants and coaches in over 60 countries, I've seen what works and what doesn't work when it comes to using video.

Over the past 30 years, I produced a feature film, several documentaries, thousands of videos, conducted hundreds of interviews and live events.

But the thing that I'm most excited about is I've produced hundreds of webcasts and earned more than a million dollars in a single day three times over and hundreds of thousands of dollars on many other shows. By the time you've finished reading this chapter, you'll have a pretty good idea of how it's possible for your business and I'll share some of my best strategies that you can use in your own business.

What Can You Use Webcasts For?

Webcasts can be used for any business, anywhere in the world and in any language including health, nutrition, fitness, business, training, financial services, personal development, coaching, consulting, business-to-business, business-to-consumer or anything you can imagine.

If you have a product or service and you can do one or more of the following:

- Talk passionately about a product or service (yours or someone else's)

- Show what the product or service is

- Describe or demonstrate how it works

- Interview a customer or client who has successfully used it

- Provide pictures, charts or graphs about the product

benefits

- Show pictures or videos of "before and after" use

- Have clients or customers who need help marketing or selling products and having you provide webcasts as a service or consultant

...then webcasts can work for you too.

Some of my celebrity and bestselling author clients who use webcasts include:

- NY Times #1 Bestselling author, JJ Virgin in the weight loss, health, nutrition and fitness markets

- Star of the movie, "The Secret", brain-training expert and NY Times #1 Bestselling author, John Assaraf

- Jordan Belfort, also known as "The Wolf of Wall Street"

- And dozens more

Why Are Webcasts so Effective and What's the History of Webcasts?

For as long as people have sold things, merchants have been searching for more effective ways to persuade and influence other people to buy their products.

They might go from door-to-door, stand on a tree stump on the side of the road or a busy boardwalk. Anywhere there's an audience of one or more people.

The more attention-getting, engaging, entertaining, interesting the "barker", pitchman or salesperson is, the more they sell. If the product was put in front of the right audience, at the right time, for the right price, a lot of money can be made in a very short period of time.

In 1984, the United States FCC made it legal for businesses to buy 30 minute segments of time on television to broadcast commercial content.

That's when the television "infomercial" was born.

In the early days, a business could produce a 28 and ½ minute program, buy time on a TV network and play that video to thousands or even millions of homes in a region very affordably and at specific segments throughout the program, tell a viewer to pick up the phone to place an order for a product.

One television infomercial, played over and over again could make millions of dollars.

My friend, Joe Sugarman, was one of the first people to perfect the television infomercial format and sold over 1 million "BluBlocker" sunglasses on TV in the 1980s.

Another friend of mine, Tim Hawthorne, built a business producing television infomercials for companies like Time Life selling music, home improvement products, gadgets and more.

And my friend Kevin Harrington sold over 500 million dollars worth of products from his "As Seen on TV" channels and launched the careers of notable infomercial pitchmen including Tony Little and Billie Mays.

My friend, Dean Graziosi, has sold hundreds of millions of dollars in real-estate training programs and has aired every single day for over ten years on TV. He's still using television - but has shifted his focus to using webcasts because they're less risky and more targeted and personal than an infomercial.

How Did I Get Started with Webcasts and Experience My First $1,000,000 Webcast Day?

Ever since I was a little boy, I've been absolutely fascinated and captivated by pitchmen at state fairs and anyone who had the magical powers of grabbing attention and converting crowds into buyers of products.

The moment it was possible to put video on the internet, I did everything I could to get deconstruct infomercial formulas and get introduced to the early infomercial pioneers like Joe, Tim, Kevin and Dean to interview them and try to understand how to adapt the television infomercial to work on the web.

That led me to producing my own "how to" information products and trying to figure out the formula to making a million dollars in a month, week or even a day.

In 2004, I produced my first Information Product, "The Internet Infomercial Toolkit" and taught other entrepreneurs how to make their own online infomercials.

In the early 2000's, you could record videos and play them back from a web site. It was expensive to host videos – but you could still make a lot of money because video was automated and sold like crazy if you knew the psychological selling secrets.

My hosting charges in those days were thousands of dollars per month.

When YouTube launched at the end of 2005, it became possible to put videos on the web for free – and the other bonus was those videos helped you get ranked and found in the search engines.

Now I was making more money - and keeping more too because the costs decreased dramatically.

In 2010, uStream, one of the first commercial services made it possible to do live streaming video. My company started to test webcasts to sell our products online.

It worked. On May 11th, 2010, my team and I produced a webcast where nearly half of all the viewers of a program bought our products that sold for $2,000-$3,000 each.

We sold $3.1mm worth of products in a single day. Until recently, I had never heard of anyone breaking that record.

It cost us $18,000 to broadcast to an audience of approximately 3,100 people for 12 hours.

In 2014, YouTube added "YouTube Live" to their service offering. It's now possible for anyone to do webcasts from their phone, tablet or computer to hundreds of thousands of people (they say even millions) for FREE.

Once again, the barrier of entry just got easier.

That means YOU can start your own online TV show, network or infomercial channel for your business or someone else's with a budget of zero.

I've dedicated my career to teaching other entrepreneurs how to use webcasts to promote, market and sell their products.

What Can You Use Webcasts For?

You can use webcasts to:

- Sell products and services

- Produce podcasts – live or recorded online TV shows

- Make video information product

- Do interactive online meetings

- Build a personal or corporate brand

- Produce interviews

- Demonstrate products and services

- Broadcast any live event

...or practically anything you can imagine...

How Do You Produce a Webcast?

To create a successful and profitable webcast, you need these five following essential components:

1. OFFER - a product or service to sell

2. MARKET with a problem to solve or a need and MONEY to buy your offer

3. CHANNEL – this is where you're going to broadcast your show. The channel I like is YouTube Live because it's free and can take on a limitless number of viewers

4. MESSAGE – also known as a "show flow" – it's a script that describes what you say in a specific order that's designed to persuade your audience

5. AUDIENCE – whether it's an audience of 1 or 1,000,000, you need to have people present to watch your show!

To build an audience, you need to get people to sign up for your event – you need to get traffic from somewhere – that's your MARKET.

The best way to build an audience (in order of value) include:

- Existing Customers

- Past customers

- Existing prospects or non-buyers

- Affiliate or joint venture partnerships (someone else's customers)

- Speaking at live events

- Books - Amazon Author Pages - Amazon Event Pages

- Podcasts

- Social Media - EventBrite - Tumblr – Blog Pages, etc.

- Paid Traffic

- (Google/YouTube, FaceBook, Yahoo, Bing, Twitter, Retargeting)

- Traditional Media / PR

To get that audience to show up, you need to invite them to register their name and email address on a lead capture page and send them a reminder email.

We use lead capture and autoresponder systems and tools including:

- Instant Customer

- LeadPages.net

- ClickFunnels

- Aweber

- InfusionSoft

- WebinarJam (http://www.PaulColligan.com/Webinarjam)

There are hundreds of services for making lead capture

pages... (just search for "lead capture page" in Google).

Here are some examples of some very successful "lead capture" pages:

74% of the visitors who reach this page click the button and fill out a form to get a free book and register to watch the videos.

This is another example of a very high-converting lead capture page:

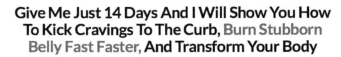

Over 70% of the visitors who reach this page click the button and fill out a form to watch the webcast with JJ Virgin and Mike Koenigs.

On the day of the webcast, an email message gets sent to the registrants with a link to a page that looks like this:

This is your "tool" that displays your video, allows the viewers to share the page with other people who might show up to watch you, a way to chat with you and ask questions or make comments and the all-important BUY BUTTON.

This page can be built by anyone who has basic HTML experience.

The Store That Never Stops Working for You

A typical webcast "show" lasts anywhere from 1 to 12 hours (no kidding!).

Most people who hear this don't believe it when we describe the duration of a webcast, but it's true. We've found that the longer the show lasts, the more sales we get.

Think of it like this:

If you owned a store and sold $500 products and it was the end of the day but you had dozens of people standing in line at your cash register, with money in hand, waiting to give it to you, would you turn them away and go home?

I hope not.

Once you practice and get good at producing engaging webcasts, that's exactly what happens.

So what happens in a typical webcast that make people want to buy a product?

The answer is really very simple – if you've ever watched an infomercial, sat in a sales presentation, bought a car or invested your money in anything, you've been through the process.

Here are the things we include that make people want to buy:

1. An introduction – welcome the viewer

2. Ask them to introduce themselves in the chat

3. Tell them what they're going to learn or experience

during the show

4. Explain the big benefits – and the opportunity (lose weight, make money, start a business, feel better, look sexy, get smarter, save more)

5. Demonstrate the product

6. Show before and after pictures or videos

7. Interview successful customers or clients for social proof

8. Interview experts or authorities who boost your credibility

9. Answer questions

10. Ask for the sale!

And then you repeat this process over and over again until the orders stop coming in or the viewership drops.

What's great about this process is if you do a webcast that's successful, you can replay it with live chat and use it over and over again. My friend John Assaraf uses this business model extremely successfully.

Final Words and Inspiration

I've spent over 25 years studying influence, persuasion, deconstructing marketing strategies, infomercials and campaigns and I've only given you a taste of the possibilities and potential for what you can do with webcasts.

The most important recommendation I can give you is if this message resonates with you and you feel you could benefit from using webcasts in your business, just open up your laptop and start broadcasting.

The more you practice, the better you'll get and I genuinely believe it's the one of the most valuable (and profitable) skills and talents you'll ever learn.

Getting in Touch and Several Free Bonuses to Help You Get Started Webcasting

If you'd like to watch a video presentation of me demonstrating the tools, technology and psychology of a webcast that was shared in this chapter, I encourage you to watch a free video presentation I made, "21 Keys to a Million Dollar Day" when you visit this web site:

http://www.PaulColligan.com/WebcastToolKit

And if you'd like to learn some of my best strategies for how to make a great looking and sounding interview, you can get a copy of my 8th #1 bestselling book, "How to Be a Video Interview Pro: 25 Strategies to Get ATTENTION and Make Your YouTube, Livestream, Google Hangouts, Skype Interviews and Videos Look or Sound Like a Professional TV or Radio Show" free when you visit:

http://www.PaulColligan.com/VideoBook

And if you'd like to learn more about Mike, head to:

http://www.PaulColligan.com/Koenigs

What's Next at YouTube?

As I hinted at the beginning of this book, YouTube has made some changes in the last year that have, quite honestly, surprised me - so take my predictions here with that understanding. I can't stress enough the power of registering the book as described in "About This Book" so that when the changes, predicted or otherwise, show up, I'll make sure you're kept up-to-date throughout the year.

It's always fun to guess as to what's coming next on any platform. In many ways, we have no more idea of what's coming to YouTube than Johnny Cash knew what was coming to rock and roll when he recorded his first tracks at Sun Records.

We will continue to be surprised and if we're smart, we'll roll with the punches and make the best out of what comes down the path. That being said, there are some obvious directions that YouTube is heading in that you should take into consideration as you plan. They fall into the categories of a Social Reboot, Premium Content Growth, More Ultra HD Content, 360 Degree Videos and more Integrated Commerce. We'll examine them all here.

A Social Reboot

Social integration is the future of the internet. All types of content will be tightly integrated into social networking: media, text, search, commerce etc. If you think about it, it makes total sense that social integration is so powerful. People care far more about what their friends think of something than does what Google puts at the top of a search topic. It's not the issue of what Google lists as the best Chinese restaurant in town; you're interested in the one that all your friends keep talking about.

Right now your results in Google are based almost entirely on whatever social tracks you've let Google get access to. When I search for something I get results different than my wife does. This customization is good for me and it is the direction in which everything is heading. You'll be seeing more and more of that type of social tracking in YouTube searches.

It's vital to keep this in mind for future YouTube Strategies because you'll need to consider the social aspect in everything you do. Design your videos to be shared for maximum impact. A Facebook strategy which includes your YouTube videos will bring you an audience bigger than your search strategy ever will. Making a video live without pinning it to Pinterest, or sending out an appropriate Tweet, will soon become a thing of the past.

To date, what we've seen with Google+ is only the beginning of the social integration we'll be seeing with YouTube in the future. With Schmidt's revelation at the beginning of 2014 that his biggest mistake was missing the rise of social media, we can all bet good money that there is plenty more to come in this sphere.

We're going to see a reboot because, simply, Google needs it and Google can afford it. Google+ was/is not enough and Google has to develop and implement a plan B - *if they want to survive.*

Acquisition targets should also not be ignored. The Google war chest is considerable and they have proven historically that they have no problem buying technologies or the companies who make them.

Continue to take note of your social strategies and how they integrate with YouTube.

Premium Content Growth

In the last year we've seen great success from the "cable killers" on SlingTV and HBO Now. People are more and more willing to spend their money on content they think is worth paying for.

Today, you can purchase and rent movies directly from YouTube. You can also subscribe to a number of Premium Channels if you are so inclined.

YouTube also has Paid (Premium) Channels akin to a HBO-type model where you can pay anywhere from $1.99 to $9.99 a month for content not otherwise available. From the Jim Henson Company to the UFC, these Paid Channels will continue to grow in numbers and in audience. In an earlier chapter, I describe how you can be part of this emerging trend.

The common assumption today on the Premium Channels at YouTube is they continue to be a fluke and that no one will pay for content that they can get for free otherwise.

However, they said the same about cable television when it first began. How big is your or your neighbor's cable bill this month?

More Ultra HD

In February 2014, Netflix launched Season Two of their highly acclaimed series House Of Cards) in 4K Video. This is an Ultra HD format akin to what you see on digital projection screens at most movie theaters these days.

Ultra HD is here (yes, you might have to buy another television set). Not only has YouTube announced support for it, but major media properties such as Netflix are already producing content for it.

What's fascinating is that YouTube actually will support the upload and streaming of UltraHD video. Yes, the impact of this capacity is, at this time, tiny; but in 10 years your HD content might look as out of place as those VHS tapes once uploaded to YouTube with such fanfare.

Here's a link to a great video that explains 4K Video quickly and comprehensively:

http://youtu.be/29TLSTGrGSQ

Here's a link to a great video that explains why some YouTubers are/were wary of 4k:

http://youtu.be.daESY7ohEwk

Regardless, Ultra HD is here to stay and we're going to see a lot more of it this year.

360 Degree Videos

Today, YouTube supports a 360 degree video format that lets you view the video from any angle. It's not a perfect technology and is currently only supported on the browser. The audience embracing this new technology doesn't seem to have passed the fascination stage at this point.

Are there strategies to embrace this year in the 360 degree video arena? No. This is an issue of wait and see.

My favorite 360 video to date is from friend Robert Scoble - https://www.youtube.com/watch?v=xjJruiWkuKY

Integrated Commerce

It has gotten very little attention, but even now YouTube has some integrated commerce capabilities. You can link from your YouTube video to iTunes and Amazon if you have content to sell there, or even to your own store at the popular ecommerce platform Shopify. http://www.PaulColligan.com/Shopify

You'll see more of this in the future. Watching a video and being able to click to buy what you're seeing has long been the dream of many media companies.

It is only a matter of time before this becomes mainstream. YouTube Cards (see previous chapter) are also expected to help spur growth.

Will There Ever Be Another?

I believe the Internet is mature enough now that there are certain players we can count on being here for the long run. YouTube is here to stay.. Yes, there was a time when some couldn't predict a life without MySpace; but I think we're at different place now.

My recommendation is to play YouTube at its own rules for the long game, considering all of the predictions made in this chapter. It's a very good bet that it'll be around longer than you will.

On the other hand, don't be foolish. Keep an archive of everything you've done, external to YouTube, just in case.

So, What Do You Do Now?

Produce the best quality video you can both in format and content and take the time required to upload it to YouTube, even if your audience can't consume it today.

Before you click the record button on another video or go live with a stream, consider the social and commercial implications and opportunities for what you can do now.

Keep a copy of everything because we can never completely predict what's ahead.

More Lessons From Johnny Cash

When Johnny Cash first recorded at Sun Records, he had no earthly idea of what rock and roll would bring in his lifetime. I believe the change coming to the internet that you'll see in your lifetime is even bigger - to the point where one day, we won't be able to recognize the YouTube that I am writing this book about.

But, just like the iPhone that Johnny Cash could never have dreamed up, the future of YouTube and your content is a very good thing - if you focus on the content.

My goal here for this book has been to give you ideas that will work in the long run. I've stayed away from screens and menus so that you think about YouTube in terms of strategies - not matching your content to however their interface might look at any given time.

YouTube has gotten to where YouTube is today because of the content. I think YouTube has handled YouTube quite well.

It's your job to think about the content.

Be strategic about everything ...

Paul's Favorite Tech

I keep a list of my favorite software and hardware at http://www.PaulColligan.com/tools . A lot of this is straight from there, and it will often be updated before this book is.

This is a list of Hardware and Software services I recommend (at least at the time of publication).

The next chapter, "Additional Web Resources," is about reference sites should help round out your knowledge.

Hardware

Camera - Canon VIXIA HF R500 -
http://www.PaulColligan.com/camera

I almost didn't put this in here because your choice of camera should be based on what you want to do with it, not on what someone else is using. Right now, my work is all done either on this camera (actually, an earlier version - this one is even better), or the one on my iPhone. I put this here to answer the "what camera should I get?" question. My one rule for a camera, though, is make sure you have a microphone jack - don't use the camera mic.

Microphone - Desktop - The Blue Nessie -
http://www.PaulColligan.com/Nessie

If you are recording audio from your desktop, this continues to be my favorite microphone right now. It's USB, works with Mac and PC and does special processing that makes your voice sound much better than it should. It's my go-to microphone for anything on the desktop.

Microphone - Lapel - Audio-Technica ATR-3350 - http://www.PaulColligan.com/lapel

As with the cameras, this is a choice for specific tasks; so I offer this microphone as one option of many. This lapel mic is good enough to be put into any camera with a microphone jack. Mine is plugged into my Vixia right now.

Software

22s.com - http://www.PaulColligan.com/22s

22s provides amazing tools for integrating YouTube Live and Hangouts On Air events into your Facebook pages. The real power of the tool is the Pro version that provides alternative options if your audience happens to be connecting on a mobile device.

Wirecast Free - http://www.PaulColligan.com/Wirecast

One of the most popular software products for live streaming is Wirecast. Whereas the product traditionally costs a few hundred dollars, there is a free option than can be used for both Google Hangouts On Air and YouTube Live.

Webinarjam - http://www.PaulColligan.com/Webinarjam

If you are involved in the world of Webinars and have used products like GotoWebinar or Webex, you've probably wondered how you could harness broadcast options provided by YouTube with the community and interaction capabilities more traditionally associated with such Webinars. Webinarjam is a new product on the market, but is extremely intriguing and worth a look.

Shopify - http://www.PaulColligan.com/Shopify

Shopify is an extremely competitive and powerful

ecommerce platform that has the unique benefit of allowing links directly via YouTube Annotations. They also have a 14-day free trial so you can make sure it is what you are looking for.

NEW FOR 2015: Tube Buddy - http://www.PaulColligan.com/TubeBuddy

YouTube automation and channel building through a browser (Chrome) plugin. Provides more power than I've ever seen in a YouTube tool and it does it legitimately. This one is mandatory.

Tube Assist - http://www.PaulColligan.com/TubeAssist

Essentially, the old standard "Tube Toolbox" (product) in the cloud, which is not only a smarter idea but also provides an option for Mac and mobile users. I no longer recommend Tube Toolbox now that this option is available.

Video LC - http://www.PaulColligan.com/VideoLC

This web-based service provides a series of tools that you can leverage to get more views on your YouTube videos. Also discussed in the "YouTube Automation" chapter.

Camtasia - http://www.PaulColligan.com/Camtasia

The original screencasting program. Works on Windows and Mac. It all started here and they continue to make improvements all the time.

Screenflow - http://www.PaulColligan.com/Screenflow

A more robust, Mac-only screencasting program. Used by many of the top names in screencasting.

Services:

LegalPodcastMusic.com   -
http://www.LegalPodcastMusic.com

Provides music with FULL RIGHTS To use in your Podcasts, videos, and more. A small fee gets you a library of music that you haven't heard everywhere else - and full rights to use the songs in all of your videos - streaming or live.

FancyHands - http://www.FancyHandsCoupon.com

An on-demand army of virtual assistants is your for just a few dollars a task with FancyHands.com. Use them for research, deal hunting, or anything else that you can think of so that you can continue to focus on your content and your YouTube Strategies .

If you have any thoughts or questions about recommendations, feel free to post a comment at http://www.PaulColligan.com/Tools . It's my go-to source for adding new recommendations.

Additional Web Resources

Putting together a list of "Additional Resources" for the tremendous world of YouTube is a daunting task indeed. Moreover, the cruel nature of the internet almost insists that the second I offer a link to the world, it will go bad.

But I want to make sure you have everything you need to build the right set of YouTube Strategies ; so with said disclaimers, I offer this list of additional web resources (see the previous chapter for my recommendations on hardware and software). I offer them in alphabetical order so as not to hint to any specific preference in any of these links.

Start Here

http://www.PaulColligan.com

How could I not?

Going Deeper Within Google+ And Google Hangouts On Air

https://plus.google.com/+RonnieBincer

Ronnie Bincer is my go-to default guy of all things Google+ - specifically in the Google Hangouts On Air sphere. He has a premium private membership site worth its weight in gold, but he also offers tremendous insight for free all over Google+. This link will take you to his profile page and you can jump to whatever you want from there.

Going Deeper Within YouTube

http://www.PaulColligan.com/Courses

I can't not mention that I'm building a few higher-level courses about YouTube that might be of benefit to someone looking to go deeper. I'll keep you up to date with everything I'm up to there.

http://www.YouTube.com/Creators

YouTube's description is best: "Your home for resources to help create better content, build fan bases, and turn your creativity into your career". If you're looking to build a career by being a YouTuber (as opposed to using YouTube in your career), there is no finer destination.

https://www.youtube.com/t/community_guidelines

If you don't stay within the YouTube Community Guidelines, they can (and will) shut down your account. Be familiar with these guidelines and review them on a regular basis.

https://www.youtube.com/static?template=terms

YouTube's Terms Of Service are a fascinating read and vital to anyone looking to take YouTube seriously. They can be changed at a moment's notice and need to be reviewed on a regular basis just in case the game changes.

Going Deeper Within Social Media

http://www.SocialMediaExaminer.com

Mike Stelzner's Social Media Examiner is my go-to guide for keeping up with the world of social media and how it all comes together. Mike's weekly Podcast is a must-listen and, occasionally, they even let this guy publish a word or two there... http://www.socialmediaexaminer.com/tag/paul-colligan/

Now What?

A good strategy starts with asking the right questions and getting the right answers. My goal here was to give you the answers to the questions I'm most often asked, while offering the best strategies for YouTube; hence the title of the book. I do believe I've done that.

I've rearranged the book a bit this year to give you a more complete understanding of my favorite online social video platform. I stand by everything I recommend here, and I promise to update these recommendations if circumstances require. I don't want to make this another pitch for registering your book but... I can only provide you with updates if I have a way to reach you with those updates.

In putting together the 2015 edition of this book, I've been reminded about how much I love this platform. The power of getting your message out (and LIVE if you want to) to almost any connected device on the planet using Google's infrastructure is pretty exciting - and infinitely powerful to anyone with a message. I hope some of that excitement has been passed along in this book.

I consider myself pretty social online. Here's how you can reach out to me through the social networks. And yes, of course YouTube comes first ...

http://PaulColligan.com/YouTube

http://PaulColligan.com/GooglePlus

http://PaulColligan.com/Twitter

http://PaulColligan.com/Facebook

http://PaulColligan.com/Pinterest

If you want to see what else I'm up to in the world of the written word, you can check out my author page at Amazon:

http://www.PaulColligan.com/Amazon

What will 2016 bring? Probably, a version of this book called YouTube Strategies 2016 - with a ridiculous offer to everyone who registered for the digital version for this edition. It's hard to give a crazy offer on print editions... but I'll do what I can if I go down that path.

"Successful people ask better questions, and as a result, they get better answers."

Tony Robbins

"The best way to say anything is just to say it."

Johnny Cash

Bonus Chapter - What Is Podcasting?

YouTube is by no means the only option for video distribution. In addition to the other YouTube competitors of Vimeo, Daily Motion and the like, is the world of video podcasting.

A large number of video producers don't realize that you can, in fact, podcast video content. As you develop your YouTube strategy, the ability to get your content out to a larger audience with video podcasting is worth considering.

My book How To Podcast 2015 starts with a chapter called "What Is Podcasting" that I thought I'd include here for you.

What Is Podcasting, From How To Podcast 2015

Podcasting is, quite simply:

Audio or video made available online for both easy on-demand consumption and/or subscription-based delivery.

That's it.

You were expecting more, weren't you? Others have certainly tried to make it out to be more than that. Of course, there are details and nuances, but that's podcasting in a nutshell.

Yes, it is simple - but there is power in simplicity.

That's it. The whole Apple, iTunes, iPad, iPhone podcasting thing - is possible because of the fact that it's *audio or video made available online for both easy on-demand consumption and/or subscription-based delivery.*

But it's not just an Apple thing. What about the podcasts on a Google device, a Microsoft phone, a connected car stereo, or some other platform out there which supports podcasts? Those too are simply *audio or video made available online for both easy on-demand consumption and/or subscription-based delivery.*

This isn't a platform thing. One single podcast will work on any device looking to access your content. You don't need to make things specifically for an iPad, Android Device, connected car stereo - or anything else.

Once your podcast is up and running, it works on any device and for anyone looking to connect with your content. In that way, it is just like radio or television - it doesn't matter if they get your content on a Sony or Hitachi device. What really matters, in fact, is that they do get your content.

How come others make it so complicated?

There are a number of possible reasons why others have tried to make podcasting more complicated than this definition. They range from conspiracy level *"they can't charge you as much once you realize how easy it is"* to human elements of *"some are so excited by the tech that they want to share with you every single element of it - even if you don't need it."*

I'll be honest, when I was first putting this book together, I posted this definition online to a few podcaster sites to see what they thought. If someone had a simpler way of explaining the process, I certainly wanted to share it with you.

I was able to refine the definition a bit, and I'm happy with how we've defined it; but trust me on this - there are a lot of people with definitions much more complicated than mine.

No matter the reason for others making it more complicated,

this book is about making it so simple so that, in the end, you can get your podcast up and running - and sooner rather than later.

So, I'll say it one more time - podcasting is, simply, *audio or video made available online for both easy on-demand consumption and/or subscription-based delivery.*

That's the definition which this book follows and the process which we outline in this book. It is the process that is going to get you up and running with your podcast in no time at all.

Let's look at our definition with a bit more focus and clarity:

Audio or video ...

Almost all audio or video media is digital now and conversion is easy for the few pieces that aren't yet digitized. The important benefit of digital media is that it's stored on a hard drive or chip somewhere, not in a warehouse (or on store shelves) with a distinct physical copy for each and every person. The same scale that quickly made Apple the biggest retailer of music is now the force behind your message. How cool is that?

As technology has gotten better, digital media has improved as well. This means that the files are getting smaller and smaller in size (making them easier to send over the internet) and getting higher and higher quality (meaning they look and sound better). Oh, the joys of technology.

... made available online ...

Because your media is placed online, it's accessible to anyone with a connection to the internet. Because the internet is almost ubiquitous now, accessing your content isn't a question of "Apple versus Windows" or "iPhone versus Android" - it's available anytime, anywhere, to anyone who knows where the content is.

... for both easy on-demand consumption ...

Yes, it needs to be made easily accessible; fortunately, that is incredibly simple to do with the existing podcasting and traditional web infrastructure. The great part is that you pay NO licensing fees to make your media available to the world... and everything that you're going to need in order to achieve that global exposure - at minimal cost - is included in this book.

Okay, so there are no licensing fees for podcasting, but what does it cost to make your audio and video available to the world? There are options to distribute this easily-accessible content to the world for less than the price of a large pizza each month. We'll discuss that in more depth in Step Two. You just might notice in our bonus section that one of the biggest names in podcasting is going to give you your first month for free, just for picking up this book.

... or subscription-based delivery.

Finally (and this remains one of podcasting's biggest strengths), your content needs a subscription option, so that when someone finds that they really like your message, they can subscribe. This means every time you release a new episode, they'll get it, automatically, 100% spam-free. This is not an iPhone or Smart TV feature and neither is it owned by Apple; this is, quite simply, the backbone of podcasting... and you can set it up very quickly.

Not everyone uses the subscription element of podcasting and that's actually a little sad. Once someone has found content they like from a source that they like, it's imperative that you make sure they're aware that they can get new episodes automatically, usually with just the click of a button.

Is That It?

Is that it? Is it really so simple?

Yes. What's more, in this book, we'll cover EVERYTHING you need to get your podcast up and running. We'll even get it to you in just four simple steps.

If you're looking for something more complicated, you're not going to find it here.

Let's get to it!

Books And Podcasts By Paul Colligan

Let's certainly not stop the conversation here. Below are a few of my other books, a Podcast or two, and a chance for us to connect "socially." And then, to finish it all off, one last reminder to register the book ...

Books

How To Podcast 2015: Four Simple Steps To Broadcast Your Message To The Entire Connected Planet ... Even If You Don't Know Where To Start

The Podcast Report With Paul Colligan Transcripts - Episodes 1-15: Complete Transcripts And Mindmaps From The Podcast Report With Paul Colligan

Cross Channel Social Media Marketing

Podcasts

The Podcast Report

Thinking Out Loud

Catch Paul Socially

http://PaulColligan.com/Facebook

http://PaulColligan.com/Twitter

http://PaulColligan.com/YouTube

Make Sure To Register This Book

YouTube will continue to change this year and I want to keep you updated with those changes. The only way I can do that if if you register this book at

http://YouTubeStrategiesBook.com.